The View From
My Wheelchair

The View From My Wheelchair

An Irreverent View of My Life with a Progressive Neurological Condition

Ted O'Hare

Library of Congress Control Number:		2023911942
ISBN:	Hardcover	979-8-3694-9251-2
	Softcover	979-8-3694-9250-5
	eBook	979-8-3694-9249-9

Print information available on the last page.

Rev. date: 06/27/2023

To order additional copies of this book, contact:
Xlibris
AU TFN: 1 800 844 927 (Toll Free inside Australia)
AU Local: (02) 8310 8187 (+61 2 8310 8187 from outside Australia)
www.Xlibris.com.au
Orders@Xlibris.com.au
851298

CONTENTS

Foreword

June 2022

This book is meant to be an irreverent and humorous look at disability through the eyes of a person who has a disability. For me, this is caused by a degenerative neurological condition, hereditary spastic paraplegia (HSP), which has resulted, so far, in significant mobility issues, requiring the use of a wheelchair.

The condition is serious, and the symptoms are very obvious. Each person's experience of the condition and their reactions to it is different. In no way do I mean to diminish or minimise the impact this condition and other disabilities have on others. While symptoms can be similar, many external and internal factors affect how a person copes with the physical impact of their disability as well as how they deal with other people's attitudes and reactions. We are all unique and deserve to be treated as individuals and with respect.

I am fortunate my family and friends, employers, medical practitioners, mobility organisations, and the local community are very supportive of me, and I have had the resources to make the modifications to my home and car to reduce the impact of my condition. Others may not be so fortunate.

There are many places where information about disabilities can be accessed. The information provided is usually accurate and informative. It is also mostly factual, unemotional, academic, dry, and impersonal, which can often make it difficult to relate to.

I intend to provide an insight into my experiences with my progressive condition. I hope it will inform and provide value to those with similar conditions. Most of all I wish to present a perspective on the impact on me and my slightly amused take on what I am going through. I am certainly not intending to provide solutions, therapy, or exercises to treat the condition. Although I have HSP, I am not qualified to offer advice on minimising its impact or effects.

I will use terms not generally acceptable, but widely used. I don't intend to offend anyone with these terms, but if I do, I am not overly concerned. Profanity may also appear. Again, I am not concerned if anyone finds this offensive. I have discovered Microsoft Word throws up the odd warning to say, "This word may offend your reader," which is really funny in itself. Perhaps it will be renamed as MS Word Nanny.

I hope you enjoy reading this because I intend to enjoy writing it.

September 2022

Writing a book takes a lot of time. It is very easy to dive down a rabbit hole and get lost before coming back to the main theme. This occurred and has required serious editing to remove my ramblings and experiences that have little or nothing to do with my HSP.

I would also add, because of my attitude regarding my ailments, my supportive family and friends, and that I have been working in the health sector for nearly 30 years, I am not despondent over having HSP and living with the limitations. I am not unique in this. Many people who have HSP or other neurological conditions or have a spinal cord injury (SCI) have a positive outlook, and although living within the limitations imposed by the condition, they are not despondent or bitter. There are, of course, people with similar or other conditions that impact their lives, who may not have the benefits I have, and so the impact on them will be very different from mine. I am aware some people with similar conditions are experiencing a much more difficult journey, so my comments and observations in this book are purely from my perspective and relate to my circumstances.

In writing this, I have discovered I seem focused on bathrooms and access to toilets. On reflection, that is because these are the areas that have caused me the most inconvenience when travelling. It is acceptable to go without a shower for a day or two, but when you need a toilet, waiting is often not an option. Other areas that cause concern are mostly resolved by the goodwill of other people deciding you can live without climbing that flight of stairs or by the use of a credit card.

The thing I have discovered as I write is, despite my intention of an irreverent and humorous take on my condition and experiences, much of what I write about is neither humorous nor irreverent. In fact, we have made a lot of significant discoveries as we have travelled. Most of them, if not funny, are not necessarily negative, but mainly highlight the generosity, compassion, and willingness to assist many people have shown me.

January 2023

I am grateful and appreciative of a friend who has been proofreading my scribblings, commenting on the content, and making suggestions about improving and changing what I have written. My wife Sonja and my daughter Erin have also performed a difficult but necessary editing job and corrected my sometimes slightly inaccurate recollections and reined in my ramblings and off-topic anecdotes.

This has helped me look at the writing in a more objective way and, I think, made the document more relevant and readable.

My goal in writing this is to have it read not only by other people living with, caring for, or working in the field of disability, but also those people who just wish to gain a better understanding of life in a wheelchair, and I hope what they read helps them by providing a slightly different view of what we are going through. If not, then I will be happy if it is read and some amusement is derived from it.

Introduction

This book is about my journey from a so-called normal person through to becoming aware something was not quite right with me, the eventual diagnosis of a degenerative neurological condition, and becoming dependent on a wheelchair for mobility. I describe how this has impacted me and my family and the changes that have become necessary for daily living, working, and travelling.

I have taken a slightly humorous view of my experiences and my observations of other people's reactions to people in wheelchairs, working life, travel, fitness, and generally what it is like living with and managing this condition.

Acknowledgements

When creating a book such as this, it is necessary to get assistance from others, and I have been fortunate to have had several people provide advice and encouragement to me. I would like to thank a number of people who have assisted me with this book.

My wife Sonja has provided encouragement, advice, and space to write the book, while also plying me with coffee, snacks, and the occasional glass of wine. She is also a highly competent proofreader and has provided much needed advice on making the book more readable and consistent. My daughter Erin has also provided editing services and helped improve the readability of the manuscript.

Tim Pegler and Anton Donker have provided advice and constructive feedback on the book and have helped with comments about how it reads, relevance, and detail.

Adele Appleby has provided much of the humour and encouragement to write the book and has kept aware of the progress of the writing and suggestions about what could be included.

Xlibris have also provided assistance and valuable insight into publishing and marketing a book.

Preface

Because of this neurological condition, I have become a full-time wheelchair user. I was having difficulty finding information from a positive perspective about living with a progressive disability. Information about hereditary spastic paraplegia (HSP) is mostly written from an academic or medical viewpoint, which tends towards a complex and factual narrative for consumption by other academics or medical readers.

A number of HSP support and research organisations are available around the world, and in Australia, the HSP Research Foundation, HSPersunite, provides excellent information about living with HSP and the research occurring in Australia and around the world.

I have written this book about my journey from becoming aware something was not right, through the initial diagnosis, and then the progression of the condition.

Without minimising the impacts of HSP on my mobility and the effect on my family, I am looking at the impacts as far as I can from a positive and humorous viewpoint.

I discuss my experiences with the condition, other people's reactions to it, the way many people view disability and the way people, including complete strangers, go out of their way to help.

I do offer some advice on planning for a trip, if necessary, but basically, this is my story on the journey so far.

A Little About the Author

Ted is an ordinary bloke who was born in the 1950s and has led a fairly normal life in New Zealand and Australia. He was diagnosed with an uncommon neurological condition, hereditary spastic paraplegia, in his late 40s, which has slowly reduced his mobility, where he now relies on a wheelchair to get around.

Ted has worked in information technology for over 40 years and in the health sector for 30 years. He is a musician and plays in a couple of big bands in Melbourne, Australia.

He has a positive outlook on life and has managed his HSP with humour and practicality. He has not allowed the condition to become the sole focus of his life, and although there is a serious aspect to the condition, he knows there is nothing that can be done to stop the progression, so feels there is no value in looking for something or someone to blame or to be angry about.

Ted has led a typical life—marriage, children, mortgage, career (work), and most recently retirement.

This is his first attempt at authoring and is a result of encouragement from the many people who know Ted and have persuaded him to tell his story and provide a less academic view of the condition.

Chapter 1

My Condition

I have a genetic condition known as hereditary spastic paraparesis (HSP) or paraplegia.

I also think my version of it is slightly different from others who have it because I do not experience a lot of pain, which I know others with HSP do. I am grateful for this.

HSP is an uncommon condition, and some would say it is rare. For those interested in understanding a bit more about the condition, there is an excellent website in Australia from an organisation known as HSPersunite. This is the home of the Australian HSP Research Foundation that raises funds to further the research into HSP with an aim to finding a cure. As with most rare diseases, there is not a lot of emphasis placed on finding a cure or a treatment for it by the big pharmaceutical companies. Rare diseases are so named because not a lot of people have the condition, which implies the market for a treatment or cure is not very large. Pharmaceutical companies are, after all, in it for the money, as they have shareholders relying on them to make a profit. I don't blame them for that; it's just a fact of life.

It is thought the incidence of HSP is about 7.5 in 100,000, based on the latest figures, June 2022, which extrapolates out for Australia to approximately 1,775 people with HSP. HSP is often misdiagnosed, with some cases being very mild or not diagnosed at all. It is often diagnosed as multiple sclerosis, cerebral palsy, primary lateral sclerosis, or similar, so it is likely the incidence of HSP is underrepresented.

There is no test such as blood test, Xray, or MRI to identify HSP, apart from gene-testing, which can identify several genes known to cause HSP, but there is no other test that can confirm the diagnosis. The only way a diagnosis is identified currently is through observation from a clinician who has experience of HSP.

My reaction to being diagnosed with HSP is interesting, looking back on it, after having the condition for 18 years. The initial symptoms as I discuss here were very mild and, initially, did not impact me all that much. My father also had some difficulty with walking, and I had seen how he had been affected, but I had not connected the dots to conclude this was what was in store for me. My emotional response had not kicked in yet, and I was not thinking ahead to what the further deterioration would be. I was treating the symptoms as I would measles or chicken pox, something you work through but eventually get over. I had some foot drop, but that would resolve itself surely. Academically, I knew what the outcome was likely to be, but while I had the mildest of symptoms, I did not concern myself with how things were possibly going to progress.

A friend of mine once said now is not the time to worry because there are only two things that could happen; this will either get worse or get better. If it gets better, there is no need to worry; if it gets worse, there is no point worrying about it now. Initially, this is how I saw HSP.

As the name suggests, this is a hereditary condition, which I am almost certain was passed on to me from my father. My dad also had difficulty with walking, although this appeared in his mid-60s and was officially diagnosed as MS by his GP.

When I started showing symptoms, I contacted my mother to find out more about Dad's diagnosis and what his symptoms were like. He had passed away, and I was trying to get access to his medical records to see how his symptoms compared to mine.

Mum gave me the contact details of Dad's doctor, whom I got in touch with. He was not very helpful at all; he told me my father had MS and that I could not get access to the medical records. This was disappointing and reaffirmed my opinion of this doctor who had failed my parents. His response had seriously upset me, and although I was not his patient, his lack of empathy and his dismissive manner seemed at odds with his role as a general practitioner. Not being sure how to proceed, I contacted my mother again and let her know the doctor was no help. Mum told me she would see what she could do, and within a few days, Mum had managed to get copies of Dad's test results and reports from some specialists Dad had seen, which she sent to me. When Mum got fired up about something nothing, nobody got in her way.

The reports from a neurologist in Christchurch were interesting, and although not a firm diagnosis, MS and HSP were identified as possible causes of his gait issues. This was the first time we had heard HSP mentioned in relation to my dad. No one had ever brought up the possibility with Mum. At the time, there was no way to confirm HSP, so MS was what the GP focused on. In hindsight, this would appear to have been incorrect, although my feelings on the matter are less generous.

My father manifested these symptoms more than 25 years ago, and there was no gene-testing in Australia or New Zealand back then. By the time I started displaying symptoms, there were testing capabilities in Belgium. Only three genes were tested for and at a cost of up to $10,000, with a two-year wait for results. I did not see this as an option for me.

Gene-testing has come a long way since then and can now identify over 80 different genes known to cause HSP. I have been tested, but the gene that causes my HSP was not identified.

Although the gene-testing has not identified which gene is affected in me, I will be tested again when the additional genes are identified and included. Finding the gene that has caused my HSP will not change my diagnosis at this point or my treatment; however, if the gene can be identified in me, then each of my children and siblings can choose to be tested to see if the mutated gene is present in them also. This would be a game-changer for them. If it is present, then they can plan for the future, but if it is not present, then they will never develop the condition and can stop wondering every time they stumble if this is the beginning of it. Which brings me to another point about HSP: There is no rhyme or reason to when you will develop HSP. Some develop HSP as children, others as teens, and others later in life, which appears to be how my family experiences it. If you have the gene, you may develop it if you live long enough. Dad's symptoms started when he was in his 60s. Mine started in my 40s. One of my adult children could develop it tomorrow, or they may not develop any symptoms 'til their 80s or at all. At that point, it might just be put down to "old age." In that way, you can see how the disease can often be misdiagnosed.

It is possible to eradicate HSP from the family, if we know which gene to test for. In my case, what we do know is my HSP is autosomally dominant. This means the gene causing my HSP was present in only one parent. If they can identify the gene through testing, it is possible to eradicate HSP from the family. Some other causes of HSP are through a recessive gene, which requires the gene from both parents to reinforce the gene which may cause HSP to be triggered.

Thankfully, research and support groups are active around the world, and there is a great deal of sharing of their findings across these organisations.

There is also a great Facebook support group for Australia with about 550 members. This is a terrific and supportive group of people who either have HSP, care for someone with HSP, or have HSP in the family. It is one of the places we turn to for advice, support, and encouragement. We learn about and share our experiences and ask questions. It is very enlightening to read about other people's experiences with HSP and the various ways this condition affects different people. We have get-togethers of group members in different locations around Australia from time to time.

I also think that, for me, if I have to have a genetic disease, this is one of the better ones to get. As my neurologist told me a number of years ago, I will die with it, not of it. Interesting choice of words but clearly tells me HSP is not a terminal condition.

We all know we are going to die. It is unavoidable. At 65, I am also far too old now to think I will live forever, but I should have a few years left yet. My wife has a lot of fun with me about my slow but steady decline. Admittedly, there are a few years between us, but she has recently taken possession of her father's house and has decided, when I die, she will sell our house and move into her father's. I am confident my demise will be through natural causes, but Sonja is a very organised person, and things are scheduled and put into her calendar. So far, I have not seen any dates for moving into her family home, but I am checking regularly, just in case.

I first noticed my gait was changing when I started catching my toes occasionally when I walked. It was just a slight catch of the toe, and I put it down to the Melbourne bluestone footpaths and roadsides or that I had maybe a glass of wine or two. I later learned this was the early start of foot drop, which is a symptom of HSP. Basically, this is where the foot does not lift fully when walking, resulting in your toes catching as you step. I learned, when a person walks, the toes clear the ground by a millimetre or two, which is why an uneven surface can trip anybody, even if there is only a small difference in height. For a person who has foot drop, the tripping can occur on a completely flat surface but is compounded if there are differences in the levels, such as height differences between paving stones, tree roots under the footpath, as well as stones, twigs, etc, on the footpath.

As the foot drop progressed and began occurring quite frequently, it was mentioned to me by a work colleague on our way to a client meeting in Hobart. He said it looked like I had been drinking, even though it was only 8:30 in the morning. He asked me what the problem was and that my stagger was getting more noticeable.

I decided, if my walking was being noticed by people and I was also getting concerned by it, I needed to do something about it. I saw my doctor about catching my toes and my stagger, which at the time were my only symptoms, and he observed me as I walked along the corridor. He told me I walked like an old man and referred me to an orthotist, who made me some inserts for my shoes. These helped for a while, and I did walk much better, but the foot drop never completely went away.

Over time I found climbing stairs was getting a bit risky, and I did stumble a couple of times.

A couple of years prior to this, I had been to an optometrist and found I needed reading glasses. It was also discovered my optic nerve was an unusual colour and I had no sight in the top left quadrant of my vision and suggested I see my GP to discuss the findings. My GP was concerned because the symptoms displayed were most commonly found after a stroke. I also discovered having a diagnosis of a possible stroke causes widespread panic in the medical profession. A range of tests were scheduled, which included CAT scans, MRIs, and a stress test. The result was, at some time in the distant past, I had a stroke. I had no recollection of having a stroke, and despite seeing I had the scarring left by the stroke, there was no way of finding out when it might have occurred and could have been many years ago. As it transpired, these scans and tests were very helpful when identifying why my walking abilities were changing.

It was several years later when I started the early symptoms of HSP, and I wondered if there was a relationship between my foot drop and the stroke. However, with the changes to my gait I was experiencing, I knew something was not right with me but did not know what it was. I had concerns that I may have had another stroke, or it could be Parkinson's, multiple sclerosis, maybe motor neurone disease, or any number of other diseases I had yet to hear of.

I went back to my GP a few times, and he reassured me I did not have MS because the scans I had when investigating the stroke would have shown the scarring on the brain that identifies MS. He had no answers for me and referred me to a neurologist to see what the problem might be.

My wife and I saw the neurologist, who specialised in Parkinson's disease. He asked me a few questions, watched me walk, decided that I did not have Parkinson's disease, and suggested I come back in six months' time to see how things had progressed. We asked him if there was anything I could do in the meantime because waiting six months did not seem a good strategy. Our thoughts at the time were he was not very interested and that he could look again after six months, and he may be more interested then. I was expecting to be provided with a strategy to fix the walking issues, medication to address whatever was causing the gait changes, and some reassurance that there was a treatment and this will get better. He was a little surprised at the question and said, if we wanted, we could get a second opinion and recommended another neurologist. I was less than happy with him, so I made an appointment with the second neurologist. When I saw him, he ran some nerve-conduction tests on me, watched me walk, and advised me I probably had HSP. Once again, this was "probably" HSP, but he did not say this was HSP. It was like everyone I had seen was not prepared to commit to a diagnosis or identify what it was I had.

Looking back now, after learning more about HSP and its diagnosis, I was quite ignorant about neurology and neurologists. I have now realised identifying an obscure neurological condition amongst the hundreds known and further determining which it is when the symptoms are common to several is not a simple thing to do. This is further compounded when neurologists specialise in one or two conditions.

I was fortunate the neurologist I went to for the second opinion, although specialised in multiple sclerosis, knew about HSP.

I was also recommended to see a pain management clinician who could advise me on medications that could assist with managing HSP if that was what I had.

I had my initial meeting with the pain management doctor, who asked me to walk around a bit; he did the reaction thing with tapping my knees and measuring the time it took for me to respond, fired off a bunch of questions about my walking and other bodily functions, which I answered. He looked at me and told me I had HSP. He also added he has seen more HSP patients in his practice than any other doctor in Australia and went on to explain what may happen in the future. He was the first doctor who told me what the condition was, whereas the others I had seen had only said it might be HSP. Although the process had taken more than six months, it was a relief to be able to name what I had rather than only knowing what it might be.

The other thing I learned was there was no treatment for HSP, apart from stretching and baclofen to reduce spasticity. He also advised me it was degenerative and progressive, which meant what I had now would only get more pronounced but could not be reversed. Just how far it would progress cannot be known because it manifests differently, depending on the gene causing the condition.

As already mentioned, knowing which gene is causing the HSP would provide a clearer idea of how the condition will progress, but because I do not know which gene was the cause in my HSP, the future progress was not known, and I had no concept of what my future with HSP would look like.

Unexpectedly, things progressed quite quickly. Not only the foot drop caused me to stagger, but also catching my toes had caused me to fall a few times. It was clear I needed help with keeping my balance and avoiding falls, so I started using a walking stick to help me when I was walking. Using the walking stick helped prevent falling and also allowed my arm and shoulder to take some of the weight off my legs, which also helped my balance.

Several years earlier, I had been given a walking stick for my 40th birthday by my work colleagues as a joke about getting old. I started using this stick, which worked for a short while, but it was too short and only for show, and although helped initially, it was not strong or tall enough to do what was needed. I purchased a taller and more robust walking stick, which helped me a lot more than the first one I used.

I was told about a physiotherapist, who specialised in neurological conditions, and I started seeing them. After a few sessions and various exercises, they recommended a slightly taller walking stick, which would match my height and would be better for me. This, I did and used it for several years.

I continued seeing physiotherapists for a while and did the exercises they specified. I did find over time that some of the exercises became more difficult, and so eventually, I stopped seeing them. This was also because of the cost of the sessions and, at the time, the almost-imperceptible benefits I was experiencing. In hindsight, this may have been premature, but at the time the exercises did not appear to be slowing the decline in my walking, and with no known way to reverse the effects on my gait, I questioned the value of continuing the program.

As I continued using the walking stick, I found myself leaning on it more and more and was increasingly putting weight on it. Over time this started impacting my shoulder, which was becoming mildly painful. I noticed I was increasingly tired and feeling worn out by the end of the day.

It was at this point I knew I needed more assistance with my walking. I decided to purchase a walking frame and started to use it around the house. The frame proved to be quite good and helped me with walking but also doubled as a seat, which allowed me to rest when needed. I still used the walking stick at work, but at home, I was only using the walking frame.

Ultimately, I did not use the walking frame for very long because I found my shoulders were still taking most of the weight, and I was leaning on the walking frame to move my legs.

In reality, the walking frame was as hard on me as the walking stick had been, and I was now finding the strain on my shoulders was becoming more pronounced, and my ability to walk was deteriorating quite rapidly.

I needed to work out how I was going to reduce the strain on my shoulders but still be able to move around. It was obvious my walking was not going to improve, so I had to find out what I could do next and what equipment may be necessary.

Once I had reconciled my ability to walk had reached the stage where I was risking a serious fall as well as increasing fatigue, not to mention my increasingly painful shoulders, it became apparent I needed a wheelchair. This would make moving around easier as well as much safer. These decisions were a little difficult to make because by starting to use a wheelchair, I was moving further along the slippery slope to being disabled. It may seem odd, but in my mind, I was the same person I had always been, but at the same time, I was becoming less. There are probably many psychological explanations for how I was feeling about needing to use a wheelchair, but for me, I was looking at my independence and perception of myself being diminished. My emotional side has found it difficult to accept the degeneration and the speed with which it has occurred. My practical side, on the other hand, understands I must address my diminished abilities and take the steps necessary to protect myself from further injury.

My first wheelchair was purchased from a local shop that catered for aged and disability needs. By a lucky coincidence, we had won a few hundred dollars in the Tatts lottery that month and when working out what to do with the extra cash, thought, *Hey, why not spend it on a wheelchair?*

There are many options for wheelchairs, but I did not know much about them at the time. The main thing I needed was something to sit on, which would allow me to push myself by using my arms on the wheels. If you have ever had a good look at a wheelchair, you will have seen the larger wheel has a ring around the outside. This is used to push the wheels around with your hand. This is called the hand rim and is fitted to wheelchairs designed for being self-propelled, meaning you push yourself in the wheelchair. The one I purchased was a reasonably priced collapsible manual chair. It was quite heavy and functional and made getting around much easier.

It was a basic wheelchair, and although I could use the hand rims to propel myself, it was more suited for someone else to push the chair from behind. However, not knowing much about wheelchairs, this did not occur to me until I had been using it for a while.

I had a couple of problems when using this wheelchair on some hills. I was travelling a bit for work at the time and regularly found myself in Sydney. For those of you who don't know Sydney, it's not built on a flat plain. Although I tried to preplan my route, if I took a wrong turn around Sydney—and my sense of direction isn't great—I often needed help in getting up the hills. On one occasion, luckily, this was generously provided by a very helpful person who was unloading some chairs and saw me struggling to get up the hill. This did highlight the fact that the wheelchair was not the right one for me.

In the end, one of the supports on the back of the chair snapped. I had a friend make a temporary repair, and I started to do some research into wheelchairs. This was my first initiation in the "technical" aspects of purchasing a wheelchair.

I contacted a company situated relatively close to where I live and booked an appointment with them to discuss my broken chair and what my options were.

The salesguy and owner was in a wheelchair himself, so I felt fairly confident he would know more about my needs than the person I bought my original chair off, who was, ultimately, just a salesperson, albeit with some training. This new salesman advised they were unable to permanently repair the broken support of my current wheelchair as it would never be as strong again and could, therefore, collapse at any time.

He asked some questions and made some recommendations as to what could suit me. I was also able to try out a number of different chairs that made a big difference. It allowed me to actually "feel" the difference between the chairs.

I ended up buying a light, collapsible, and simple-to-maintain wheelchair, which suited me very well.

By this stage, I was only able to take two or three steps using the walking stick.

After using that wheelchair for six years, I now have another wheelchair made to suit my mobility needs as well as my physical requirements. While my second wheelchair was still "off the shelf," this third one is essentially a "bespoke" wheelchair. Before the wheelchair was designed for me, several measurements were taken. These included my height, the length of my thigh, the length of my lower leg from the foot to the knee, the height of my shoulders from my waist, and the length of my arms. This means the seat is a bit longer to accommodate my long legs, and the seat itself is slightly higher so I have a better position for the hand rims. It is also made of a lighter metal, titanium, so it is not as heavy to push or collapse and store in the boot of the car.

About a year after getting this wheelchair, I lost the ability to walk completely, so I am totally reliant on the wheelchair to go anywhere, but more on that later.

As I have already mentioned, each of our experiences with HSP can be dissimilar, and others have symptoms quite different from and many far "worse" than mine. I don't experience a lot of pain, whereas many others need to deal with significant and often debilitating pain.

Some forms of HSP are classed as "complex" and include other symptoms, such as hearing or vision loss or dementia. Some people have their hands and/or arms affected. I am hopeful my disease does not develop these other complex conditions. My father did develop dementia, which meant he eventually had to move into a care facility, where he stayed until he died. I have been assured by many people who know nothing about HSP that HSP and dementia were unrelated. I sincerely hope this is the case because I mildly panic every time I forget a name.

I imagine, if other symptoms develop, we will deal with them as best we can.

Chapter 2

Day-to-day impact

I consider myself to be lucky my wife has been on this journey with me and has been the absolute rock that has supported me through everything that has come our way. Although I am the one who has HSP and displays the symptoms, it is a condition that has an impact on my entire family, and Sonja takes it all in her stride. When necessary, she explains what is happening with me to our friends and relatives and others we meet. She also handles all the other shit that comes our way, be it her autoimmune conditions or our children's health conditions and treatments. She has a natural tendency to be a mum to everyone, which many people at her place of work benefit from, but she is also ready to reprimand them when required. She has an enormous capacity for loving and caring for many people and the ability to throw out the "suck it up, princess" commentary when needed.

One of the things I love about my family is I am me, and they all treat me as their father, husband, partner, or whatever. One of the things they don't do is pander to my disability. They help me when I need it, but for the most part, I do whatever is required, and to a large extent, this is expected. The conversations we have about my wheelchair use are seldom unless it is pertinent to our plans. Everyone has some issue or problem they cope with, and one of mine is HSP and an inability to walk. It is just a bit more noticeable than other people's issues.

In some ways, it is a good thing all of us in my family have an appreciation of disability and many of its forms. For us, there is no concern or nervousness about a person with a disability because to various degrees, we all experience it in some way, directly or by association.

I do admit to having an understanding but not a lot of sympathy for those who have a disability that becomes the sole focus of everything they do and talk about. There are a number of people who have a "woe is me" take on things, and I feel, to an extent, some lose the perspective that life continues, regardless of your condition. There is still a life to live, and it is necessary to look beyond the limitations imposed on you by a medical condition and keep working towards the future. I think perhaps my attitude is more positive than some, but again, I am in a very loving and supportive family. Other people may not be and can be quite alone and unsupported. I do feel for them.

Despite, this there are times when things catch up on me, and my enthusiasm and optimism take a hit. There are times when I have had enough of climbing in and out of the wheelchair, when I am stuck somewhere, and know, if I could take three steps, I could get to where or what I need. This is particularly true when what I am trying to get to is the wheelchair. If it is out of reach, I am staying where I am. How can the wheelchair be out of reach, you ask. Occasionally, when I am sitting in my comfortable recliner, watching the TV, another person will come into the room and sit down. They discover my wheelchair is blocking the view or is in their way, or their natural mischievousness comes out, but it results in my wheelchair being moved away out of my reach. This is usually followed by everyone leaving the room and me having to shout for someone to get my chair for me. Moving the chair away is necessary at these times, but once it is moved, it is no longer front of mind. Moving it back again so I can reach it is not thought of because if you don't use a wheelchair, why would you? This does, of course, help me maintain my "grumpy old man" persona, which is increasingly more difficult to achieve.

There are times when I am trying to get out of bed, but it is taking a long time and considerable effort to sit up and transfer into the chair.

This is a frustrating aspect of my condition but one I have mostly become accustomed to.

One of my pet peeves and a source of frustration, but also can be highly amusing, is trying to put my trousers on when sitting down. Have you ever tried to do that? Until recently, after putting both feet into the trousers, I could stand up and quickly pull them up as I slowly collapsed backwards onto the bed. I can't do that any longer and have discovered it is far more difficult to pull up your trousers when you are actually sitting on them. Now I have to wiggle from side to side to hoist my trousers up so my modesty is intact when out in public.

This is also true when needing the toilet. As you all know, it is necessary to remove your trousers and underclothes before completing your task. Now try to do that and transfer from the wheelchair onto the toilet, complete the business, get your undies back up, transfer back to the wheelchair, flush, and then wiggle around while pulling up your trousers; then wash and dry your hands and move on so the next person in the queue can use the loo. This is not a very quick process, but it is impossible to avoid. Attempting to delay the task can be extremely embarrassing as you can probably imagine.

When transferring into my wheelchair, I also find my trousers slide down my bum so the belt ends up in an uncomfortable position, where I am half sitting on it. This is particularly true when transferring into the car from the wheelchair and again from the car back into the wheelchair. The different heights tend to drag my trousers where they shouldn't be. It is also a little difficult to adjust them back to a more comfortable position unless I undo them so I can wiggle around to pull them up properly. Unfortunately, this is not acceptable in polite society, so an alternative method had to be found. When out with Sonja and this occurs, I ask her to work her magic for me. This means I stop the wheelchair, and she moves in behind me, I raise my bum off the seat using my arms, and Sonja will reach down, grasp my trousers on each side, and hoist them back up to where they should be. This fixes the problem, is socially acceptable, and assures my comfort until my next transfer.

I, along with many people with HSP, find the temperature has an impact on my symptoms. I don't know if everyone with HSP experiences this in the same way, but I do know I much prefer warmer weather, and for me, winter and HSP are not good company. I feel the cold, particularly in my legs and feet. I now use an electric blanket in bed if the night is cool. I used to detest an electric blanket and did not use one, but I now have it on regularly, even in summer, if the night is not warm. Sonja does not feel the cold, and at times she will be feeling too warm wearing a tank top and shorts and will put the cooling on while I am having to put on a jumper. I have bought an electric throw rug, which I now use when I am cold. From my knees down, my legs are often blue and cold to touch. My feet are often many shades of blue.

I have asked my specialist about why my legs are cold, and the explanation was my internal thermostat no longer works because HSP stops the messages from getting from my legs to my brain. This means my legs are behaving as if they are warm, and the blood flow is reduced, thereby making them feel cold.

It's funny how things progress, and you never know what may cause the "next stage." I was having a shower at home recently, and part of the process includes transferring from the wheelchair to a bench put into the shower as part of the badly needed renovation shortly after we moved into the house. One of the things that happens because I am in the wheelchair full time is that my legs get used to being bent in the seated position. When I transfer in the shower, I have a fitted handrail I hold on to. On this particular day, when I stood up to transfer, it felt good to straighten my legs, and so I stood and stretched a little. My legs felt great for a moment, but they then decided they had had enough and simply collapsed. The result was I fell between the wheelchair and the shower bench and quite painfully wrenched my shoulder. After resting there for a time feeling sorry for myself, I decided I did not need a shower that badly after all.

I now had to get up off the floor and back into my wheelchair and check for damage. It took a while to accomplish this and would not have been quite so simple if my wife had not come in to see what was taking me so long. She had to assist me with getting back into the chair without doing any further damage to my shoulder. My daughter was also willing to assist, but because I was naked, this was not necessary. Seeing a parent naked could have a lasting traumatic impact, so it is best avoided.

My shoulder was quite painful, and I discovered it was not much use to me. No matter how I tried to use it, the moment any weight went onto it, the pain was severe, and my arm collapsed. Transferring to or from anything was suddenly much more difficult.

Panadol and Neurofen were necessary additions to my medicine routine, but it became painfully clear I needed to find a better way of transferring from my wheelchair to another seat as necessary and back again. With some experimentation, I did find my good arm was OK for weight-bearing and my sore arm was OK for balance and holding on to things to steady me, but no weight could be applied. There were a couple of mishaps where I almost embraced the floor again but luckily, did not do so.

After a couple of days, my shoulder was still quite painful, so I decided I needed to get a medical opinion on it to see if I needed to get some treatment. I made an appointment with my GP.

I have been seeing this GP for a number of years, and we get on quite well. He is a sports medicine specialist and was able to check out my shoulder as a sports injury.

We went through the process of checking for damage to my shoulder ligaments, tendons, muscles, bones, and rotator cuffs, which determined there was no "serious" damage but it would be sore for a few weeks. You may find it surprising, but I actually hadn't seen my GP for well over a year at that time. There is nothing he can do for my HSP, and like most men, I tend to not need regular visits when nothing is wrong. With him being a doctor who wishes to see me frequently to feel needed, he wanted to do the usual checks, such as blood pressure and my general health and book in that cholesterol test, which I never did get around to when life became interesting with the pandemic.

He hooked me up to his blood-pressure machine, which does the check and presents the results. Obviously, his machine needed attention because an error message kept coming up on the screen, which confused the GP and amused me.

He decided he would go back to the old-school way of checking my BP, so he got out his stethoscope, put the cuff on me, blew it up, and then slowly released the pressure, and we got a pretty healthy BP reading. At this point, he decided to check my pulse rate and proceeded to do so. That's when the penny dropped for him as to why his machine kept getting errors. Apparently, my pulse rate was all over the place, like a drummer gone mad, and it was difficult to get an accurate reading. This had nothing to do with HSP; it was just another curve ball life throws at you.

Suddenly, the number of bits of paper I was going to take away with me started increasing. He explained I had an erratic heartbeat, which was the reason his BP machine was giving errors, and I had what was called atrial fibrillation. Basically, the top part of my heart was going nuts, and the bottom half was trying to work twice as hard—the atria were doing a shit job, and the ventricles were trying to keep me going.

Anyone who has been diagnosed with a condition requiring a specialist to treat it will understand that you are suddenly thrown into the medical system, a system that envelopes you in a warm and caring embrace and introduces you to a whole raft of medical aficionados who have your best interests at heart. You then travel along the route going where you are told to go, seeing who you are told to see, and listening as the "experts" lay out your future for you. They tell you what will happen to you if you follow their instructions and what terrible consequences will occur if you don't. You will most likely be given a whole slew of medicines you have never heard of, and you will come away with a definitive set of instructions on how and when to take them. At least that is what happened to me. Interestingly, you are not consulted about what is happening to you, but you are told what will happen and what the treatment will be, but you are not expected to say anything in return and definitely not encouraged to ask questions.

Since my initial appointment with my GP, I have met a lovely sonographer who did an ultrasound ECG. I have met a bubbly and happy nurse who fitted me with a Holter monitor to wear for a day.

I also met a cardiologist who gave me an idea of what was happening with my recalcitrant blood pump. He even drew me a diagram of what my heart looked like and where the different bits were located and what they were supposed to do. I proudly showed this diagram to my family who immediately decided that my heart looked like an arse.

The cardiologist, whose art projects at school obviously did not make it to the fridge door at home, decided on a course of action, and so I soon headed off to the local hospital for a day procedure, where they zapped my heart with electricity to reset the rhythm, much like performing a reboot on your computer.

Once I arrived at the hospital, I was taken into the day procedure unit, where I was anaesthetised, put to sleep, for a short while, maybe five minutes, and while asleep, the surgeon stopped my heart and then shoved a few zillion volts through it. I have a vision in my head of the dead parrot sketch from Monty Python. This worked, and my heart started up again and resumed its normal rhythm.

In other words, I went to hospital where they killed me and then brought me back again.

Now I get to continue with my suddenly numerous medications, which are going to thin my blood, reduce my cholesterol, slow my heart rate, and lower my blood pressure. Oh, and not to forget, I also have new meds to help heal my shoulder, and I still have HSP, so all these meds are in the mix now.

Another aspect of the procedure is that yes, it worked, but there are no guarantees it will stay that way, and it is possible that the mad drummer may return.

The good news, for me at least, is I went home from the hospital with a well-behaved, steady, and rhythmical timpani beating in my chest. So far, it seems to have worked because I am still writing this, and my newly discovered ECG app on my smartphone now says sinus rhythm, which is what is supposed to happen. Let's hope it continues to do this.

In the meantime, I have a bucketload of pills to keep taking until the medical profession decides I no longer need to.

For me, an important thing to remember is, just because I have HSP, it doesn't mean I am immune to everything else. Life still happens, shit still happens, and like a lot of people with a significant disease, not everything is related to that disease. The doctor who told me HSP would not kill me has proven to be correct. It could be my heart, cancer, car accident, snake bite, or any number of things. It is just a matter of remembering to listen to my body and to not ignore what it is telling me, remembering, of course, that I am a bloke and tend to overlook what is blatantly obvious.

You have got to laugh. Several months after my fall, I did my usual gym work on Saturday, mucked about at home, watched telly, went to bed, and woke up in the early morning with a very sore midsection. Of course, I started cursing my personal trainer for causing this pain, but it was getting significant and somewhat concerning. Sonja rang Nurse-On-Call, another excellent service provided by Australian Health Services, and discussed what could be causing my discomfort. After a short while, they suggested that Sonja call an ambulance because I needed a doctor to check me out.

The ambulance duly arrived and gave me a quick check-over. They had given me some pain medication, which had very little effect, and also identified that my atrial fibrillation had returned, so a cardiac issue was suspected, which required going into hospital. A couple were suggested but previous experience precluded going there, so I ended up at one of the local public hospital's emergency departments.

I was examined, questioned, had a CAT scan, and was told my gall bladder needed to be removed. I had very little idea of what that entailed, so I had some pain medication and was admitted to a ward.

Because of the medication I had been taking for my heart shenanigans, I could not have the operation immediately because the blood thinners needed to be out of my system before they could operate. So I waited a couple of days before being scheduled for surgery. The surgeons hoped the gall bladder operation would also reset my atrial fibrillation.

On a side note, the planning for my procedure was a little complicated because my internal baclofen pump was where one of the laparoscopic incisions was to be made. There was a team planning session, and they identified an alternative route around the pump.

I was wheeled into theatre, where they dutifully removed my gall bladder. Having had a number of general anaesthetics, I was mildly surprised I had no woozy sensations as the anaesthetic was being administered, and I woke up after the operation not realising it was all over. Previously, I have needed to count backwards from 100 and generally get to 97 before everything disappears, but this time around, it was just lights out.

I woke up in recovery, had a quick check and something to eat, and was then taken back to the ward and into the care of the nursing staff. I was checked on every couple of hours; pulse, BP, and temperature taken and dutifully logged into my medical record. It appears my atrial fibrillation had not resolved as hoped, but this was not an issue for them.

This public hospital services a large area of Southeast Melbourne, and there is an enormous mix of ethnicities and language. The treatment I received from the nursing and medical staff was a lot better than what I have experienced at several private hospitals.

Some aspects of the stay were not so wonderful but in the grander scheme, mean little. The food is selected from a menu, so there is a significant selection, but unfortunately, it is very difficult to discern the difference in flavour of each of them. Even an omelette has the same texture and consistency as roast beef. The meals were adequate but definitely do not appeal to the palate.

After my wounds began to heal, I was visited by the surgical team manager and was advised, from his perspective, I could be discharged. Because I use the wheelchair and was having some difficulty transferring, because I had lost some condition and the bed height in relation to my wheelchair was quite significant, the physio team would not sign off and wanted me transferred to a rehab hospital to make sure I could continue to live at home.

Although I had definitely lost some condition, I was still able to transfer in and out of my wheelchair, and I also knew, at home, most things I transfer to are of a similar height. They were unconvinced, and so I ended up discharging myself from hospital "against medical advice" and needed to complete and sign a waiver so I could leave.

That was done, and I am now back at home in the bosom of my family, with familiar things around me and where the food is much better.

Because my atrial fibrillation had returned, I have been back to my cardiologist and will be returning to hospital again to have my heart zapped to hopefully reset the rhythm again.

I do find it mildly amusing that despite assurances that I will know when my heart goes into afib, I actually don't feel anything wrong. I am supposed to be breathless, but I am not. My heartbeat is irregular, but I don't notice anything. Basically, I feel fine, but the medical profession is having a small panic on my behalf.

Chapter 3

Family Impact

I have been married twice and have two children from my first marriage and two from my second marriage. My eldest daughter lives in New Zealand with her three children, my grandchildren, and my other three children live in Melbourne. None of them live at home anymore, with my youngest daughter moving out recently.

One of the things that has concerned me the most about having HSP and understanding its progression has been my perception of the impact this has on those I love and care about. My greatest fear that has kept me awake at night and troubled me since I started along the journey of decline has been how my condition adds to my family's worries. I know we have a love for one another, which is shown every day. As my physical decline progresses, however, I am fearful the love they have for me will change through various stages. It may start by stepping from our normal family dynamic, where my role as husband and father is known and understood, changing to become more supportive with a sympathy dynamic. It may then move on to accommodating my limitations, where I need to be looked after. I am worried their feelings for me will change further and morph to a frustration with my declining ability, devolving further to becoming my carer, and ultimately, I become an additional workload for everyone and a burden to those I care most for in this world.

I have a recollection of my father explaining his condition to someone on the phone and saying "things are OK" and that he can "still make a cup of coffee." I heard my mother's muttered reply, "Then why do you never bloody well make one?"

There is no doubt I am not as able to do things I used to do and that my wife Sonja has had to cover the things I can no longer do. Sonja is a very organised and practical person, who has accommodated my slow decline and the limitations I have accrued. She has come to terms with the fact that over time, I will be able to do less and less around the house.

I discuss the National Disability Insurance Scheme (NDIS) later in this book, but it is worth mentioning here that a number of activities I used to do are now undertaken by external organisations and are paid for by the NDIS. Two of the main ones are lawn-mowing and house-cleaning.

Many other things I can do still, and I have recently retired from full-time work. This gives me time to do these other things. It is important for my mental well-being and my sense of self to contribute to the household duties for as long as I can. In this way, I can relieve some of the load on Sonja and the family. I am learning new skills, such as cooking, which I was never very good at; keeping things tidy; folding clothes that have been brought in from the washing line; and similar stuff.

There is an incentive in doing this because despite her love for me and her support through my decline, she has always maintained the moment I cannot wipe my bum is the day I am moved into assisted living, or as she so eloquently puts it, "Out of here and into a home."

My role as a father has not changed dramatically, and I am still providing advice and regularly comment on the antics of my kids.

Each of my children have developed into wonderful adults with their interests, skills, and achievements. I am immensely proud of them all and have learned and continue to learn from them every day. They all show a deep loyalty to family and friends, a sensible and compassionate attitude to life and other people, and have followed their passions in employment and community activities.

Amongst them there are many skills and achievements, which include parenting, customer service, and retail, theatre, encompassing acting, writing, and directing, psychology and counseling expertise, and production and project management in movies and arts. They are all making their way in the world, and as a parent, it is gratifying to witness.

They live with the knowledge that they basically have a gun pointed at their heads, which one day may go off. Or it may not, and we will not know more unless the gene-testing can identify what triggers HSP in me.

Before I was diagnosed, Sonja and I purchased what we thought would be our forever, or at least our very long term, house. It was a lovely two-storey house, or a stair house as the kids put it at the time. It had views over the Dandenongs, a spacious backyard with room for a pool, a paved entertainment area out the back stairs, and was split level on the ground floor to give us wonderful high ceilings in the bedrooms.

As my mobility deteriorated, living in a split-level house with stairs up to the front door, a step up into the lounge or down from the kitchen into the hallway, as well as a whole upper level, was becoming a bit of a problem. As a result of being diagnosed with HSP, I had become a member of the MS Society, that also supports people with similar conditions, especially ones who have relatively few people affected.

My wife spoke to them about the house and my mobility limitations. The purpose of the call was to find out what their suggestions were to adapt the house to my declining mobility. They suggested we sell the house and move to a place more suitable for my wheelchair. We explained the kids were still in school and were settled, so it was our intention to stay at the house until they were ready to move out. The advice from the MS telephone service was blunt: "Stuff the kids, they will adapt, but I cannot keep living in a house that I can't get around in."

It was a light-bulb moment. It often takes someone else to state the obvious before you see it for yourself. To be honest, we had not considered this until it was pointed out to us by the MS Society. It was the obvious solution to a lot of problems.

It took us over a year to find appropriate accommodation. The house had to be single level, no steps into the house, a separate area for the kids, who were now in their late teens and early 20s, and room for a pool or already have one. We finally found one that matched enough of our needs while easily being able to be modified for the few issues it had and was in the location we really wanted. Since moving in, we have had the bathroom updated with handrails, roll-in shower, etc, and have added ramps to the back door and up to the garden gate. We also had remote openers for the gate installed so I could easily open and close it without needing to ask for help or raise myself off my chair.

This means, when everyone goes out and abandons me at home, there are no guilty consciences because I can still get out and about if I choose. I normally go with them, but often, when the trip is to pick up something from the supermarket or similar, I will stay home because it is easier than locking the house, transferring into the car, stowing the wheelchair, driving out to the shops only for me to stay in the car for the five minutes it takes Sonja to pop into the shop.

One of the things that appealed about the house we purchased was the fairly large in-ground swimming pool. We had an above-ground pool at the previous house, and it was used quite a bit by us all.

The in-ground pool is excellent; however, because the weather has not been normal for the last few years, we have not made as much use of it as we would prefer. Simply put, the weather has been good during the week when we have all been busy and fairly mediocre at the weekend. So when we have time to use the pool, we are not motivated to do so.

However, when the sun is shining and work is not calling, we do use the pool, and it is great. There is a deep end and a shallow end, solar heating, twice as much as we need because nobody wants a cold pool! And it even has a spot where the water bubbles and beats you about a bit. This could be a spa, but really it's just a bubbly seat.

Not too long ago, I was able to stagger (walk?) to the pool and sort of launch myself in. Now I roll myself to the edge then slide off it onto the ground and then down the steps into the water. Getting out is the same in reverse but without the assistance of gravity. This was doable until the end of last summer, when it became almost impossible to perform without injury or a lot of help, so an alternative had to be found.

They say necessity is the mother of invention, so we looked about for something to help getting me in and out of the pool. After deciding upon and then discarding many an idea, we settled on a simple device we already possessed that would aid the transition from dry to wet and back again. It is a very handy and well-engineered device called a step stool, which we put next to the wheelchair. I can use it as a support to get off the chair and as something to help with climbing back into the chair. It's not perfect, but it definitely helps.

It also serves another purpose, which is to provide a source of amusement and subject matter for my family to tease me. They are normally very supportive, so I forgive these moments when they lapse. Besides which, a lot of the comments made are very funny.

After a while and my fall in the shower, using the step stool became a bit of a problem, so we looked around for another solution. We found one that works well: We purchased a number of steps developed for people exercising and for doing yoga. I use them to move from my wheelchair onto a stack of these steps, then onto another stack that is lower, and from there, into the pool. This works well, and I now have three steps to transfer onto to get into the pool and the same in reverse to get back into my wheelchair.

One of my daughters and her partner recently purchased a house about an hour's drive away from my home, so we, of course, had to go and see it and give it the Dad seal of approval.

I am mildly concerned that my daughter is attempting to tell me something in the way she chooses her abode. I am sure this is not intentional, but where she previously rented and the house she has now purchased has a staircase to climb before you can get to the living area.

This was less of a problem when I could still climb stairs, but now that I am unable to do that, getting to see her new house was a mite tricky, but it was something I was determined to achieve nonetheless.

Once we arrived, we drove down to the end of the long driveway of townhouses, parked the car, and entered via the garage. My daughter and her partner had bought the back townhouse in a six townhouse

block. There is a door at the back of the garage, which leads to a flight
of stairs, which take you to the first floor, where the kitchen and living
areas are. The staircase has a banister, which I would have used to climb
the stairs, as I had done in the previous house, but climbing stairs, as I
said, was no longer an option. So I sat in my wheelchair at the bottom
of the steep stairs and gazed at them going up and up and up.

The house is three storeys with a garage on the ground floor, up the
stairs to the living area with a further flight of stairs to the bedrooms.
Looking at the stairs from the garage, it was apparent there was only one
way for me to get up to them, and it certainly was not in the wheelchair,
and I was not going to be carried. It did, however, require persistence,
tenacity, determination, and a fair amount of effort on my part.

I calmly got out of my chair and started to climb them on my
bum. In simple terms, I sit on the bottom step, use my arms to lift my
bum onto the second step, and then drag my legs onto the first step.
Repeat process until you get to the top step, whereupon I wait for my
chariot to be brought up the stairs, and then gracefully, or as gracefully
as possible, hoist myself into the wheelchair, and casually have a look
around as if I do this every day. The effect of this on those watching me
was concern, fear, and mild nervousness, initially, which slowly became
amusement and silly commentary and ended up as extremely funny,
ribald jocularity, and was followed by days of my loved ones hanging
shit on me.

Once into the living area, I was able to look around and admire the
lovely home they had purchased. With an air of wisdom and the slight
relief of everyone else, I declared I did not need to inspect the bedrooms,
which were up another flight of stairs.

After the inspection, we planned to celebrate by walking around
the corner to a very nice restaurant for dinner. This meant, of course,
I had to get down the stairs again. With the added benefit of gravity,
I proceeded to bump my bum back down the stairs at a significantly
quicker pace than the upwards one.

Upon returning to the house after the restaurant, I discovered the
driveway is a lot steeper than it appeared. Admittedly, I was assisted up
the incline going to the restaurant, but going down the hill, I found, even

with me holding the wheels so they would not turn, the wheelchair slid down the hill quite rapidly and completely out of control. Fortunately, I enjoyed the adrenaline rush and increased heartbeat, and the momentary panic resolved itself into "man, what a great trip," reminiscent of the motorcycle song by Arlo Guthrie. Then when I got to the bottom of the hill uninjured, with slightly less tread on the tyres, and the cries of anguish had faded into soft echoes, we got back into the car and went home, with yet another adventure behind us.

I, like many others, became ill with Covid but having been vaccinated, did not experience the dreadful symptoms other people had. In all, my Covid experience was more like a mild cold, but I did experience fatigue, and I was unwell.

What I was unaware of was my getting Covid caused some family members to be very concerned for my well-being. This was because I was in the wheelchair and could not stand up to move around, which, of course, meant my lungs were not expanding to full capacity. As you are aware, Covid can cause breathing issues and congestion in the lungs, and many people have died from this. I have learned since my Covid was the topic of discussion with concern, that I may have breathing issues and need to go to hospital.

None of this transpired, and I did not learn there was this concern until many months after I was clear of Covid.

Although I do not want to cause my family worry about me, it is nice to know they do and think of the consequences of me getting ill. In reality, if I am not worried about myself, then someone should be.

Chapter 4

Driving

I have driven a car and had my driver's licence since I was 16, and over the years, I have driven many different types of vehicles. I have driven manual cars of many types, including using a "crash" gearbox, a three- and four-speed column gearstick, several four-, five-, and six-gear floor shifts, and I even used a preselect gearbox once, but that was truly strange.

I had been using an automatic transmission for many years prior to my diagnosis, and as my legs deteriorated, even using an automatic was becoming a bit difficult. It was fine for a while, but once I started using my arm to move my leg from the accelerator to the brake, it was time to look at something else.

At one stage, I was driving home from work late in the evening, and my legs were not working very well, so I used my walking stick on the brake pedal because I could not get my leg across from the accelerator. Probably not the safest method, but it worked at the time, and I dismissed it as being the result of tiredness after a long day at the office.

Shortly after, Sonja and I were driving to Adelaide, when she observed me lifting my leg from accelerator to brake. After thinking about it for a while, she decided this was not a good option for me or anyone else in the car or on the road. She then took over the driving for most of the trip, making me the designated passenger.

With the progression of the HSP and my need to manually move my legs when driving, I decided I needed to investigate hand controls for the car. So the fun began.

Even though I had been driving for 32 years, I found out I had to start again. First, I had to find an occupational therapist who could assess me for driving. Then I needed a driving instructor who could teach me the use of hand controls.

Finding an OT was quite a task because there is a fairly high demand for them, and not all of them have the experience to advise on driving.

I contacted several organisations who had OTs as well as a number of individual OTs. Unsurprisingly, there were few who were able to do the driving assessments and fewer still who had availability before the next ice age. I did eventually find an OT who was recommended to me, and she explained what needed to happen for the driver assessment. Finding a driving instructor who understood hand controls was far more simple than finding an OT, so I set up a time to start my new driving lessons.

One Saturday morning, a small car pulled up the driveway, and a nice bloke got out and introduced himself as the driving instructor. We talked for a couple of minutes, and then he started fitting the manual controls to his car. As a driving instructor, he needed to be able to avoid a collision, so he needed to take control using a second set of pedals in case I couldn't drive using my hands only.

After 32 years of driving, it did take a little bit of getting used to. To accelerate, you push the handle down, and to brake, you push the handle forwards. Sounds simple, and in fact, it is. Easy as anything, in fact, until you end up in one of those situations where you need to decide quickly if you need to speed up or stop completely. This happened, and I needed to stop very quickly, but oh crap, do I push or pull the lever, or do I try to get my foot onto the brake? For a moment, I contemplated panic, but instead, I made a split-second decision and pushed the lever forwards, and the car stopped. Pulse rate up, breathing rapid and shallow, sweat on the brow and armpits, rude words escaping my lips, and a driving instructor laughing his head off, I was relieved once I had stopped, but thinking about it afterwards, it was not the driving that was an issue but familiarity with the hand controls. As the instructor said several times, if you have good driving skills, it is only using the hand controls that needs to become familiar.

I had about four lessons with him, and I totally appreciated using his car and not mine. I bumped over kerbs, turned too sharply, stopped where I shouldn't, but actually hit nothing and thankfully, did no lasting damage.

Next, I had to undertake the driving test with the OT sitting in the back and marking how I did. Suffice it to say I did well and had only one questionable comment, where I may have put the indicator on a little too soon before making a turn.

I was then free to use my car. I had it fitted with hand controls, and with a newly endorsed licence given to me by Vic Roads, I was able to regain my independence and get back on the road.

Nowadays, I can only drive a car that has an automatic transmission, has power steering, as well as hand controls and a spinner on the steering wheel. Anything other than this and I am a passenger.

Having driven this way now for over ten years, it is as natural as it was before I needed the controls.

One surprising part of running a car for me and one I had not considered is, since I have had the hand controls, I have never filled the car with fuel. I sit in the driver's seat, and my passenger gets out and fills the car. It's a practical thing really. For me to fill the car, I need to get out of the car and into the wheelchair, then I have to go round to the filler cap, unlock it, take it off, get the fuel hose, put it in the filler, and start pumping fuel. Once full, replace the hose, replace and lock filler cap, get to the cashier, pay, get back to car, get in driver's seat, get wheelchair back into the car, and drive away. Elapsed time, between 15 and 20 minutes. I am a patient person, but even I would be getting royally pissed off if the guy in front of me at the bowser took 20 minutes to fill up their tank, no matter what the reason.

The freedom the hand controls provide, however, is brilliant. Since the controls were fitted, we have driven to many parts of Australia: Brisbane and back via the Blue Mountains, Mildura, Port Campbell,

Sydney, Echuca, Adelaide, to name a few; which brings me to another point: We love a good road trip, probably more than most, but when we travel, where we stay and what we want to do there need a bit of planning and forethought.

Chapter 5

Getting About

Moving around outside the home is a very important part of living with limited mobility. If you can't walk, which I can no longer do, getting from one place to another presents some issues. This could be something as simple as getting invited to a party at a friend's place or as complicated as catching up with people at a restaurant for dinner.

None of these are of any concern to anyone whose mobility is not compromised. When it is impaired, however, there are many things that need to be understood and planned for. Going anywhere for the first time can be a little daunting, but there are a couple of things that can reduce the unknown a little.

Making a call to the venue, if it is a restaurant or such you will be going to, and asking them is the best way to understand what is available. Another way to research locations is by using technology. Google Maps and Street View are amazingly good resources to use. By using them, you can identify any physical problems that may impact you. Are there stairs leading into that restaurant? It is also good to be able to see what the streetscape may be like. Are there pedestrian crossings with lights to use, or is there a public car park nearby? Are there steps to get to a shop, or is it a ground-level entrance?

In Australia, there are some mobility-specific apps and websites that can be used to see what the access is like and what facilities are available en route. More of these are still being developed, but they are becoming more simple to use and more comprehensive.

Having access to this data means your trip can be planned and a lot of the barriers can be removed or taken into consideration.

Of course, there are always unexpected things that totally screw up your planning, such as roadwork or building sites, where the footpath has been closed and extremely steep ramps are provided to get you over the gutter. I often laugh at the signs posted, which usually say, "Pedestrians, watch your step." If you use a wheelchair, are you a pedestrian?

The interesting other one is when a large hose is laid across the footpath. It is assumed pedestrians can step over these. In my case, I have had some of the workmen come out and lift the hose so I can roll underneath it. Other times they have come out with boards to enable me to get over the hose. Basically, this is because people are good-natured and big-hearted and don't want to see a disabled person struggling if they can assist.

There are, of course, others who are not so good-natured, who probably unconsciously make it difficult for many others. These are the people who park their cars, vans, or trucks across the footpath, making it impossible for a wheelchair, pram, or even pedestrians to get past without having to get onto the road to get around them. It is also common to have motorbikes and scooters parked on the footpath, which also causes difficulty to get past, particularly when the footpath is narrow.

Most disabled car parks have a strip between them with yellow stripes marked that provide space for the cars to offload the wheelchair, walker, etc. It is not uncommon for that space to be used as a motorcycle park, a place to leave your shopping trolley, and I have horrifyingly seen it used as another car park.

While I don't believe the people who park across a footpath or the motorcycle that parks on the footpath are doing it to purposely inconvenience others, I do think they need to be made aware their actions can significantly inconvenience a lot of people. On the other hand, I think anyone who parks or uses the only place disabled people can get in and out of their cars in clearly signposted parks are not only inconsiderate, but are also consciously, purposely, and maliciously hurting people with disabilities.

I and many other wheelchair users quietly scheme and plot ways of exacting revenge upon these inconsiderate ratbags. So far, I have not come up with anything effective that won't land me in jail, but I am still working on it.

Car Parking

Car parks are an essential part of travelling, and when your vehicle has been modified, an accessible park is a necessity. Accessible car parks are those that have a blue colour with the standard wheelchair picture on it as well. You will also note a sign on a pole showing the same symbol, which will often have a time on it.

If the time says two hours, then a person displaying a disability permit can park there for two hours, after which a parking infringement notice will be tucked under the wiper blade. On the street, however, a disabled driver with a permit can park in a regular car park and is able to park there for double the time permitted. So if the car park is in a two-hour zone, the permit enables parking for four hours.

Most public car parks will have designated parking for those with disabilities. These parks are signposted and blue in colour, and they are also a bit wider than a standard car park. The reason for this is it allows for wheelchairs and similar to be unloaded from the side of the vehicle without damaging the car beside you.

Although these car parks are designed for use by people with disabilities, who have the appropriate permit displayed on their windscreen, the accessible car parks are also used as a taxi stand, as a loading bay for deliveries, parking for tradies when working on site, as a place where limo drivers can park when waiting for clients, and also where anyone can park when rushing in for a coffee, or other quick shopping need. Occasionally, a person with the appropriate disability permit can use one as well.

It is interesting to note that shopping centres and commercial car parks cannot issue fines because only governments can issue fines. There is an article on news.com.au that discusses this. It appeared on 6 February 2023.

This actually shows a person with a disability, who has the appropriate permit to use an accessible car park, has no rights in a commercial parking building, which is not subject to council parking inspectors. Even though these car parks are vital to people like me who need the larger parking space, there is no authority to enforce this in a privately run public car park.

It is an interesting observation in a council-managed parking area, if I parked in a loading zone or on a taxi stand, I will get an infringement notice; however, a truck or a taxi using an accessible park does not receive an infringement notice. This is not always the case, but I have seen vehicles parked in an accessible parking spot without showing a permit where the parking inspector walks past without looking to check if they are legitimately parked there.

I have asked a parking inspector about why this is the case, and the response was there were higher-priority issues they concentrate on. This is a source of intense frustration for disabled motorists.

At my last employer, I used the car park at Southern Cross station, which has the most accessible car parks of any public car park I have used. I have never had a problem getting an appropriate park there. Once parked, there are several lifts that can be used to get to the ground floor. I did learn, however, the lifts are turned off in the evening and are not turned on again until the morning. For me, this meant, if I worked later than 6:00 p.m. or had a function on that finished after that time, there was only one lift that could be used to access the car park. As is always the case when Murphy's law is applied, the lift operating was the furthest away from where my car was parked.

The other interesting car parking experiences are at suburban shopping centres. There are usually a good number of designated parking spots in suburban shopping centres, and normally, whenever you need one, they are all taken. It would seem there are times when people with disabilities all go out. These times seem to be over the weekend or public holiday. In fact, at our local shopping centre, on a Saturday, there are more wheelchairs, walkers, and power chairs inside the shopping centre than at any other time, and there are not enough accessible car parks available for all of them. This means many will need to park in a standard car park or park a distance away from the shopping centre.

Another aspect of using the accessible parking areas is the judgment made by others about your need for it. It is not uncommon for a person to park in the disabled car park with the correct permit displayed getting out of the car and walking into the shops. They are often accused of not needing the permit or have borrowed a relative's disability sticker to get a "better" car park. In reality, it does not matter because many disabilities are not obvious but are real. You don't need to be in a wheelchair to require a disabled car park.

I admit to a high degree of frustration when in recent times, penalties have been introduced for people who park conventional cars in a spot reserved for electric vehicles, where they can charge up. Similarly, there is a lot of noise about people parking in places reserved for prams. There is a lot less noise about people parking in spots reserved for disabled drivers.

Public Transport

I seldom use public transport now for several reasons, but the main one is where I live is not very well serviced with public transport. The only public transport in the suburb is a bus service, and while the buses are accessible, the bus stops are often inconveniently placed, and the buses themselves are often crowded.

It is also a 30-minute drive to the nearest train station, and the parking there is often fully used. A train from the station to the city is a journey of at least an hour. The trains are accessible and are very good, but the stations at either end can be more difficult to negotiate because of the number of people at the station and being able to find and use the lifts. Although the trains do have dedicated places for disabled passengers, the trains at peak times are very crowded, which is not very comfortable for wheelchair users and can make it difficult to see which station you are at to know when to get off the train.

Melbourne is well known for its extensive tram network, and now with the modern trams, most of them are accessible for wheelchair travelers. Additionally, in the CBD, many of the tram stops are raised so a person in a wheelchair can get on and off a tram easily. The downside of this is many of the tram stops outside the CBD are not raised, and it can be difficult to get off the tram when using a wheelchair.

I am sure, if I needed to rely on public transport, I could do so, but at this stage, I am more than happy to drive myself, which works well.

I don't have a lot of experience with public transport in other states; however, at one point, I was visiting some clients in Newcastle just north of Sydney in NSW. I needed to also meet with another client in Gosford on the Central Coast, which is a trip of about 90 kilometres each way. There were no rental cars available that had the hand controls necessary for me to use, and it was much too far for a taxi, which meant the only way to get there and back was on the train.

I went to the train station and tried to buy a ticket, but the vending machine was not well designed for a person sitting down, so trying to read the instructions was difficult, particularly when the sun at that time was at an angle that all I could see were reflections.

One of the station staff on the platform saw I was having some difficulty and came over and assisted me with getting the ticket. She then asked me about how far I was going and where I needed to get off the train. Then she escorted me to the train where a ramp had been organised to get me into the carriage. Once on board the train, I settled into the carriage, and the train started its trip to Gosford.

As we progressed towards Gosford, I started to wonder how I was going to get off the train again and how I could get assistance, if needed.

A lady got into my carriage a couple of stops later, and we started talking. She was asking me about my wheelchair because she had a son who was also in a wheelchair, so we ended up comparing our experiences. Her son wanted to play wheelchair rugby, and the NDIS provided the funding to buy a suitable chair for him to use. We agreed, despite its many issues, the NDIS was the best thing to happen for disabled people in recent times.

I asked her if she knew how I could get off the train when we got to Gosford, but she wasn't able to advise me; however, she did offer to go and stand in front of the bloody thing until I got off. She was a gem.

In the end, it was all so easy. The train pulled up at the Gosford station, and there, on the platform, was a bloke with a ramp all ready for me to get off the train. Seemingly, the staff at Newcastle had called ahead and let the Gosford team know when I would get there, what carriage I was in, and be ready with a ramp. It worked just the same going back to Newcastle as well, and there was a taxi rank available at each end of the trip to get me where I needed to go.

I am quite sure the same thing will occur in Victoria, if I need to use the rail service in the regional areas, but at the moment, it is still easier for me to drive.

Chapter 6

Accommodation

This is an area that is very complex and holds many dangers for the unwary. When looking for accessible accommodation, there are a few things you need to be very clear about. The first is what you need. This sounds simple, but in reality, when looking at accommodation, it is easy to assume your capabilities are more than they are. For me, anyway, I often overestimate what I can do, which has led to some frustrating situations. The other consideration is if you will be on your own or will there be someone else with you. Your needs when travelling on your own are very different from those when travelling with someone else.

The other part of the picture is what the accommodation provider sees as accessible and what you are able to do can vary greatly. It is understandable but also unfortunate that the general understanding of what a person with disability needs is some handrails around the toilet. If there are particular needs for the disabled person, these need to be identified and enquired about before booking the accommodation. In my experience, I have expected that an accessible room would also have a shower chair provided, but in a number of places, I have had to ask for them. Is the shower a wheel-in, or is there a door with a lip you need to get over?

All your needs should be understood and accommodated. If you need a hoist to get in and out of bed, then you need to find out if there is one available. If you assume there is and find there isn't, then you are the one who has the problem. These needs must be qualified first and alternatives found if they are not available.

As I mentioned, I have travelled quite a lot through my work as well as travelling for holidays with my family. The accommodation requirements are similar, but the work trips are on my own, whereas the holiday trips are filled with noisy, demanding, and for some obscure reason, perpetually hungry family members and sometimes friends.

There are many types of accommodation: hotels and all their different types of motels, inns, B&Bs, guest houses, camping grounds, cabins, and many others.

Since I have been using a wheelchair, and previously, when I was using the walking stick, I have stayed in many different types of accommodation, but in general terms, when travelling for work, I have stayed in hotels, and when travelling with the family, I have stayed in motels and cabins.

As my condition deteriorated, I soon discovered what is defined as an accessible room, which caters for people using a wheelchair, varies considerably from place to place. A hotel will generally have a number of accessible rooms, and I have stayed in quite a few around Australia. As an example, there is a lovely hotel in Sydney I have stayed in frequently, which was in an ideal location to get to where I was working at the time. It had a great bathroom with shower bench, handrails where needed, and plenty of closet space. It also had a fridge, and coffee-making facilities were on a level where a person in a wheelchair could reach them. Everything was good, and I stayed there many times. The only downside was the door into the room was a self-closing door, and once closed, you needed to be well braced and strong to open it. I was able to get the door open, but it did require some strength and an ability to brace the wheelchair far enough away from the door so it would open without the wheelchair getting in the way, but close enough so you can reach the door to open it. This was more complicated if you were checking out and had your bag with you.

Other hotels I have stayed in, which state accessible rooms, do not necessarily have accessible bars and restaurants. I have stayed in a very nice hotel, where the room was fine, but to get to the restaurant, it was necessary to go to reception and ask for them to arrange a ramp for the steps into the restaurant. Then when you have finished the meal, you again needed to ask for the ramp to be brought back so you could leave. In other hotels, it has been necessary to use a stair lift to get into the restaurant and bar area. This is fine, but as a guest, you are often not permitted to operate the stair lift. You need to press a button that summons the operator who comes to the stairs, sees that you need to use the lift, then explains that he needs to go and get the key, which he goes to find. When he returns, he climbs the stairs, inserts the key, starts the lift, opens the door so you can get into it, then closes the door. He then presses the button that moves the lift to the bottom of the stairs where you can get out and go to the table. On one occasion, this process took 30 minutes instead of the usual ten minutes or so, and I was more than ready for a drink by the time I got to the table.

Most of the time, though, the lift takes you to the floors needed. There are no issues with ramps, stair lifts, and the like. To be fair, most of the hotels that need this type of equipment are older buildings, where it is not feasible to modify to accommodate a wheelchair user.

I have also experienced the situation where despite ensuring that where you are staying will accommodate a wheelchair without a problem, once you have checked in and got into the room, there is an equipment breakdown, such as the bathroom shower seat not able to be moved off the wall or the toilet not secured to the floor, which makes it impossible for you to access things you need. At one hotel, the restaurant was closed. I could still use all the facilities of the hotel apart from the restaurant and bar. I was able to get room service, however, so I was fed and watered OK.

Many hotels use designers for modeling their rooms with different looks for executive rooms, suites, business rooms, and also disabled rooms. The design of the disabled rooms, although looking great, may not actually assist those with a disability. The room may fit the theme of the hotel, but often there are significant aspects that do not work for a disabled person.

Sonja and I stayed at a hotel in Lübeck in Germany, where the shower basically drained into the lounge because there was no real slope to the drain, and there was no curtain for the shower, so the toilet and toilet paper were wet also.

The majority of rooms I have stayed in have had little or no storage space to put any toiletries. Even my electric toothbrush falls in the sink because there is no bench space.

A very nice and upmarket hotel in Vancouver had a designer bathroom, which looked great until you used it. The bench for me to sit on when showering was too far from the taps, so I could not turn the water on when I was in the shower. If travelling alone, this would have been a big problem but was less so because I was travelling with Sonja.

We recently stayed in a hotel near to a music festival we went to. The hotel is part of a large chain and offered accessible rooms, one of which we booked. Once we got into the room, it looked like it had everything we needed, but once we started using the room, a few things showed the room was not as accessible as expected. On the one hand, the room had tea-making facilities—cups, kettle, and tea—but these were not at a height appropriate for a person in a wheelchair. The main inadequacy, however, was the bathroom. Initial inspection showed there was a pulldown bench in the shower. There was a handrail around the toilet and room beside it to accommodate a wheelchair. When I started using the bathroom, however, things were not quite so good. The gap beside the toilet was the same width as my wheelchair, so although I could get into the space, the wheelchair was hard up against the toilet and the shower screen. It did work but was a bit interesting to get in and out of.

The shower, however, was not great. It was a roll-in shower with no door, and it had a pull-down bench for sitting on when showering. Looking at it, I think the shower had been a normal room shower that had been adapted by adding the bench to make it accessible. The bench had been installed against the wall that also had the mixer control and the soap and shampoo bottles. This meant, to use the bench, it was necessary to squeeze under the mixer tap to reach the shower head and to reach behind and up to get the soap and shampoo. This did not really work very well, so I had a quick shower but did not have another until I got home. If you had a checklist for an accessible bathroom, this shower would get a tick in all the boxes; however, anyone who needed an accessible shower would not see this as accessible.

Motels are normally very good, although at times it can be difficult to get a booking. We have stayed in motels quite a lot, and for the most part, we have been very happy with them. We have always called ahead to make sure they have everything needed, but occasionally, we have found what we need and what the motel say they can provide are not quite the same thing. Often the accessible room does not have the space for the wheelchair to get around the room, or the benches are too high to reach things. For me, most of my needs are to do with toileting and washing. I cannot get into a small toilet area nor into an enclosed shower; however, I can use a larger space that enables me to transfer from my wheelchair onto the toilet or a shower bench or chair.

We have experienced motels where there is no shower chair available, which means I cannot use the shower. At one motel, we asked for a shower chair and were told disabled people need to bring their own because they do not have one. This was an oversight on our part because when we called ahead to book, we did not ask about a shower chair but assumed there would be one in the accessible room. We ended up with an outside chair being brought in, which worked, just. Quite a few motels use an outside PVC chair as a shower chair, which is OK for a one-off but not good as a regular option. They are really not that stable, and the armrests make it difficult to transfer to.

Another option we often use is to stay in a caravan park with cabins. We have stayed in these a number of times, and for the most part, they are great. There is usually at least one cabin, with suitable shower and toilet facilities, that caters for wheelchair users. Cabins also tend to be a bit roomier than a motel room and will have a kitchen area where food can be prepared. Cabins are a very good option when travelling, although depending on what time of year, they can be booked out months in advance. At holiday times, there is often a minimum stay, which may be two days or could be up to a week.

An important thing to note if you are travelling and need accessible accommodation, it is necessary to book in advance. If you are needing the room at a holiday time, this is essential. An accessible room is available to people who don't actually need the facilities. Most accommodation providers will book the accessible room as one of the last rooms available, in case it is needed by a disabled person. Ultimately, if it is vacant, it will be used. The accommodation provider needs to sell every room, every night. You would be extremely lucky, or travelling in the offseason, if you had not booked ahead and managed to get an accessible room when you showed up looking for a room. Therefore, we no longer drive until we are tired and then book into a hotel. These things need to be preplanned.

We recently travelled around the state with some overseas family, and despite a couple of minor issues with a few people, the trip was excellent and enjoyed by us all. We stayed in several different accessible accommodation places, and all of them were good and worked for me, but a couple of them did require help from my wife. This was mainly to move things, such as a shower chair, but also to move furniture away so I could access things more easily.

One place in particular had been modified to enable a disabled person to use the house, and while I did not need many of the assistive technologies in the house, they were there for people who did. These included hoists for getting in and out of bed and a chair that could be wheeled about by a carer.

There are many options available for people with disabilities to travel and stay away from home, and by understanding what your needs are and researching where you can stay, the trip will be enjoyable, and any compromises can be understood and accommodated.

Chapter 7

Camping?

Recently, some good friends of ours were planning a camping holiday and asked us to come along. It had been a number of years since we had been camping, and while I had been many times, it was not something Sonja had done a lot of. I had certainly not been camping since my diagnosis of HSP. Despite the fact that I am using a wheelchair all the time, we really wanted to join them, so we needed to have a good think about what we could achieve and what equipment we might need.

The process was further complicated by the fact that the camping spot they were going to was essentially a mate's block of land, out the back of whoop whoop! There would be no civilised amenities. Just us and the kangaroos.

Our friends have a caravan, but that was not something Sonja and I could use because I would not be able to get the wheelchair through the door, and I would be unable to move around inside the caravan. I know you can purchase or even hire wheelchair-friendly caravans; however, my car would be unable to tow one. This meant we would have to hire or buy a car as well—the dollars were starting to add up, and we didn't even know whether we would like caravanning!

The next best option would be a tent. Our friends had spent a number of years camping using tents before they splurged on their caravan. They had accumulated quite a collection of tents over the years. Sonja and I analysed what we would need to make this work.

We decided the minimum we would need would be a tent with camp stretchers I could get into and out of without too much difficulty, an accessible toilet of some description, and a shower, if it all went terribly wrong.

We were invited to our friends' place to sort out our options and found they had spent a fair amount of time and effort in setting up some ideas in their backyard. The first tent was set up with camp stretchers assembled inside. I needed to get into the tent and be able to transfer onto the camp stretcher and lie down to see if that would work for me. It worked really well and was quite comfortable. We already had a spare camp stretcher at home from one of our kids' Scout Jamborees, so Sonja could use that, if needed. Sleeping problem solved.

Another tent had been set up, and this had a temporary floor and a portable shower setup. We could fit a plastic chair under that, and as long as I had a short shower, this would also work well. Shower problem solved.

Last, there was another marquee tent set up with a camp toilet inside. They promised the marquee came with walls, and the girls proceeded to attach them. They'd had a couple of glasses of bubbles by that stage, so it wasn't a quick process and did involve a lot of—pardon the pun—toilet humour, but after a while, it was done. As you can imagine, a camp toilet is not very stable. So we took measurements and started to Google some options for a frame with a toilet seat. Discovering there were plenty, I declared it a success. Tick! Toilet problem solved.

With no more obstacles in the way, we deemed it feasible, and so we made plans to go camping.

Although there were some nervousness about it, we were all quite excited about going camping. As the time got closer, life got in the way. Sonja's father was quite elderly and became unwell, and we consequently had to cancel our camping trip. We did go up there for a day but did not stay overnight. While we had a wonderful time on our day trip, we have decided the first time we go wheelchair camping, we might try baby steps and book into a caravan park. Then again, caravan parks have wonderful cabins, so who knows? Maybe the toilet frame will sit forever, unused, in a corner of the garage.

Chapter 8

Wheelchair modifications and attachments

When you use a wheelchair as your primary method of getting about the place, you become aware of some of the compromises that need to be made. An obvious example of this is you no longer have hands free to carry stuff like a briefcase or a bag of groceries, etc. It gets further complicated because now we all carry a mobile phone or a tablet computer or even a pad and pen. These can be placed on your lap or beside you on the seat of your wheelchair, but they invariably fall off, generally when trying to cross a busy road or on the footpath, risking trampling by pedestrians striding along with their noses stuck in their phones.

To address this, we have done a little research on what you can get for your wheelchair, which can assist you with having the things you need close to hand but also not limiting your ability to push yourself around.

When I got my first proper wheelchair, it came with a net fitted underneath the chair and enabled me to put things in it. At the time, I didn't think I would have a lot to put in the net. It's not like I had a handbag full of stuff I could empty into it, or so I thought. There were my glasses, sunnies for nice days and reading glasses if I wanted any chance of seeing a menu or document; wheelchair gloves, which I quickly learned were essential; a baseball-style hat to keep the sun off my balding head; and other things, such as my laptop computer when going to work.

One of the attachments my wife has been urging me to get is a coffee cup holder, which can clip onto the wheelchair and is available whenever I need a drink. Actually, she wants two, one for her and one for me. It's all for my benefit, she assures me, but I suspect it is so she can have both hands free to play Pokémon Go when we are out and about, but that's another story! So far, I have resisted having one for a number of reasons but mainly because there are alternatives, and I really don't want to clutter the look of my wheelchair.

The other attachment I am not getting is a clip for my mobile phone. There is absolutely no way I am getting one of those. The phone can stay in my pocket or under the wheelchair for as long as my hands are working OK. I want nothing that will detract from the sleek, svelte, and streamlined look of my chariot.

One of the best things we ever did was buy a backpack for the chair. These have been extremely important when we have travelled, and I have purchased several backpacks over the years. They fit over the push handles at the back of the chair and provide a good place for putting the shopping, spare jumpers, jackets, books, iPads, snacks, hats, scarves, and anything else we can fit into it, such as drink bottles. The other essential item kept in the backpack is my set of Allen keys, which are needed to adjust or tighten things as necessary on the wheelchair.

As I have mentioned, we like to get out into the fresh air and wander around parks, reserves, beaches, riverbanks, and similar. We are fortunate to have access to a lot of these environments quite close to home, but once trying to access these places in a wheelchair, you very quickly become aware of the limitations they have.

The way most manual and folding wheelchairs are made is they have two rear wheels that are quite large. The most common is the 24-inch wheel as the big ones at the back, although they can be bigger at 25 inches or 26 inches. Wheelchairs seem to be designed and manufactured in the USA, and so most of the dimensions are in imperial measures of feet and inches. For those of us who use the metric system, 24 inches is a tad under 61 centimetres.

As you will know, wheelchairs also have silly little wheels at the front called castors. These vary in size, from tiny little wheels like you would see on roller skates and can get up to 6 inches in height. They can go larger than that, up to 10 inches, but this will depend on your needs.

The smaller the castors, the more likely they are to get caught or stopped by gravel, twigs, or stones. You have probably used roller skates, roller blades, or skateboards on the footpath at some time and hit one of these obstacles; you will remember how the wheels and your legs stopped suddenly, but the rest of you kept going. Then you hit the footpath and generally lost some skin, but the embarrassment of having your friends witness your demise was truly mortifying. It is similar in a wheelchair as the passenger ends up flying out onto the ground as the chair flips over beside them.

One of the things I have bought for the wheelchair, which has had a huge impact on the ease of getting to places we want to go, has been the FreeWheel. The FreeWheel is a wheel with a pneumatic tyre, which attaches to the front of the wheelchair and raises the front castors off the ground, turning the wheelchair into a tricycle. This prevents stones, twigs, bark, small steps, tree roots, children, and small dogs getting caught by the castors. The FreeWheel rides over these obstructions and enables you to take the wheelchair off the paved tracks and use more rugged paths.

As I mentioned earlier, we do like to get out into the parks, riverbanks, beaches, etc, and the FreeWheel enables us to do this with relative ease. Although fairly expensive, it has been one of the best purchases we have made in allowing me to go to places inaccessible to a normal wheelchair, such as forest tracks and the cobblestones we experienced in Europe.

Over the years, I discovered the human anatomy is a little fragile when having to push yourself around in a wheelchair with only your arms to do this. Legs have very large muscles attached because they are designed to carry the weight of the rest of the body over long distances and often at speed. Arms, however, were designed with no thought for replacing the legs.

I suspect, if I had needed the wheelchair when I was in my teens or 20s, I would have been able to adapt more readily to using my arms, and the musculature and other bits would have developed to accommodate the new use. However, I was in my 50s when I started using the wheelchair, and by that time, my arms were highly developed to do what arms do. Once I started pushing myself around in the wheelchair, I discovered there were some fairly significant limitations to using my arms for moving me around. I also found I did not develop huge biceps, taut abs, or a manly chest.

The most significant limitation was to do with gravity. Flat ground requires effort to move along, but it's OK. Downhill is exciting, and the only thing to manage is controlling the speed because at some point, you are going to have to turn or stop, and that needs time and distance, depending on how fast you are going.

The opposite of downhill is, of course, uphill, and there is no easy way of pushing yourself up a hill. Short gentle inclines are fine, but the longer they get, the more effort is needed to get to the top, and if the incline is steep, the harder it becomes. Simply put, your arms get too tired to push.

There is another element to consider when pushing yourself around, whether on the flat, downhill, or uphill, and that is the camber of the surface, something a person on two legs has probably never thought about. Most footpaths and roads are angled slightly so when it rains, the water runs off it. When pushing a wheelchair, however, the camber angle also pushes you away from where you are wanting to go, so you need to counteract it by steering the wheelchair against the camber. This does, however, add to the strain on your shoulders and hands, and so you tend to get tired more quickly.

I had seen an attachment for the wheelchair, which looked pretty good but was well outside my price range. This was a wheel similar to the FreeWheel but with an electric motor, handlebars, and throttle. I started looking for alternatives to this and found one that was affordable, slightly smaller, and could be very effective. After considerable thought,

I purchased this, and once it arrived, I set about assembling and installing it.

Armed with my trusty set of Allen keys and a screwdriver and my years of knowledge gained from buying from Ikea, I started putting it together. It only took about a week, and I had it finished.

I don't use it a lot, but hills are no problem now, going either up or down. The other benefits are it does not wear my arms and shoulders out, it has a range of about 40 kilometres, it has three modes for different speeds, and at its fastest, it will get up to about 30 kilometres per hour, which is exhilarating but scary in a wheelchair. My youngest daughter tried it out to see how fast she could go, and with shouts from her mother to not break it ("You mend, the chair won't!"), she proceeded to crash it into the gutter. She did, however, get it up to 35 kilometres per hour!

It also has lights, so it can be used at nighttime and a horn that can be used to warn others you are coming. I tend not to use that because it is a most insipid-sounding thing and way too embarrassing to use. It has a reverse mode as well, which sounds the horn in a beep-beep manner, the same as a truck reversing. I, therefore, limit my use of reverse and pull a U-turn instead.

This add-on is not something I use every time I go out, but if a long-distance is needed or there are many hills, it is very good to ease the effort necessary to get to places, and those accompanying me are disinclined to push me up the hills. It was very handy during Covid for our longer walks around our suburb.

Chapter 9

Air Travel

I have travelled quite a bit for work, and before my mobility issues kicked in, there were very few problems and nothing that couldn't be overcome. As a younger man, I travelled around New Zealand from Christchurch, implementing IT systems in Dunedin, New Plymouth, Napier, Palmerston North, Auckland, as well as more locally in Ashburton and Timaru.

Since moving to Australia in my 30s, I have travelled to all the state capital cities as well as regional centres across Australia and to the United States, Europe, Indonesia, and Thailand for business and pleasure.

Prior to HSP, travelling was never an issue, and even when I initially started showing symptoms, there were few problems. I would occasionally catch my toes when walking onto an aeroplane or when walking to appointments. I was once accused of being pissed, inebriated, at 8:00 a.m. After that happened a couple of times, I started using a walking stick, cane, when I was out. The accusations of public drunkenness stopped after that, which was something of a relief.

I was once walking to an appointment in St Kilda, Melbourne, when a young fella started walking beside me and talking to me about how I was walking and that I didn't really need a walking stick. He was basically having a joke with me, but I let him know he was right, I didn't need the walking stick, but it did cover up the fact that I could have a few drinks, and the stick hid the effects so nobody knew. He thought this was such a good idea that he was going to get a walking stick as soon as he could.

As the condition progressed, however, the walking stick became more essential for me to get anywhere.

I needed to use it getting on and off aircraft, and I started to learn about other people's reactions to someone who was a wee bit "different."

On one occasion, the stick was in the overhead locker, and after we landed, the person behind me opened the locker and the stick fell out onto the floor. He obviously got a fright and in a loud voice said, "This is very dangerous."

Several passengers pointed that out that upon landing, the announcement is made to use caution when opening the overhead lockers because items may have moved during the flight.

Over many flights, and some where the landing has been a bit more of a collision with the ground, I have heard the announcement to be "Please take care when opening the lockers because I can guarantee that after a landing like that, nothing is where you left it!"

I recovered the stick and let him know it was a lot more dangerous for me to not have the walking stick, but he was unamused. The other passengers were having a good laugh though.

As my mobility decreased over time, I needed to take my wheelchair on the flight with me, and eventually, I needed to use an aisle wheelchair to get me to my seat on the plane. This means I need to transfer from my chair to the aisle chair at the cabin door, and I am wheeled to my seat by the flight crew. Now you know why people with disabilities are let onto the plane first. Not so we can avoid the queue, but to stop us getting in your way as you wander down the aisle and stow your luggage in preparation for takeoff.

It did take some getting used to, but the crew are generally very good and patient, so apart from relying on someone else to get me to where I need to be, the process is simple and effective. Before takeoff, my wheelchair is folded up and taken by the ground crew to be stowed in the luggage hold until we arrive at our destination. There, it is miraculously brought back to the cabin door for me to transfer back into and get on my way. The person using a wheelchair who flies is generally first on and last off the plane. This is completely opposite to everyone else getting off the plane. It is absolutely farcical to remain seated and watch all the other passengers trying to get their luggage and get as far forwards as they can while waiting for the door to be opened and disembarkation starts. Once the plane has landed, passengers' patience disappears, so anyone not moving fast enough is at risk of being trampled by the horde behind rushing to get into the terminal. Once in the terminal, there is a race to get to the luggage carousel first so you can pick a good spot and wait for the luggage to arrive.

Normally, by the time their luggage is retrieved, they can then rush out and join me in the taxi queue.

One of the frustrations I have when travelling is I am totally dependent on someone else bringing me my wheelchair at the end of the flight. On a couple of occasions, the wheelchair presented to me at the destination was slightly different from the one I had put on the plane. The first time this occurred was not too bad. The only thing that was changed was the wheelchair had been put against something that was quite dirty, and so one side of my chair was covered in a black substance. This did nothing for my appearance once it got onto my hands and clothes, which required a trip to the bathroom to resolve.

On another occasion, with a different airline, my wheelchair was put onto the plane with two swing-away footplates as is normal, but when it was presented to me at the aircraft door, it only had one, slightly inconvenient because I still have two legs, and it is preferable to have two footplates.

The captain of the plane who was at the door when my wheelchair was brought to me went into the hold to see if he could locate the missing footplate. He couldn't find it, which he let me know when he returned. His efforts were, however, appreciated. At this point, my only option was to make my way to the lost luggage window, where an extremely helpful lady gave me a clipboard with a form to fill out, which I did, and gave back to her. Unfortunately, that was the extent of the help. In fact, there was virtually no discussion at all and certainly no apology or assistance offered. I now had to continue my journey, including my business meetings with both feet trying to stay on the one footplate left. Not so easy to do when you can't control where or when your legs fall. I ended up having to constantly stop and put my right foot back on top of the left one.

In time, my claim was sent through to a mobility organisation in Melbourne that ordered the wrong parts from the manufacturer in the USA. When I received them, I contacted the mobility organisation and advised them the parts were the wrong ones and even sent photos of what the correct part was. They reordered the parts, and eventually, the correct ones arrived. All in all, I was using a compromised wheelchair for about eight weeks before the correct part got to me.

I also received a message from that airline to say they could no longer take me or my wheelchair on their 737 services because my wheelchair did not meet the criteria for carriage and that I could only travel on their A320 services. At the time, the A320s travelled very early or very late, which basically made it impossible to travel with this airline at the times I needed to fly. The great Australian airline was perhaps not quite so great. Interestingly, though, the other carrier accepted my wheelchair on their 737 service without a problem.

I also had a less-than-satisfactory trip with the airline that did accept my wheelchair. When I returned to Melbourne after a trip to Sydney, my wheelchair did not get back to the plane for me because it had mistakenly been sent to the luggage carousel. An airline wheelchair was found for me to use, but this was not of a type I could move myself because it only had small wheels, which meant it needed someone to push it. It was a busy time, and I was "parked" in a corner of the lounge area and told they will embark this flight and then take me to get my wheelchair. During the time when the passengers were boarding the flight, one of the ground crew staff kept glancing over to see if I was still there. When the flight had closed and departed, I was still waiting to be taken to the luggage area, but there was nobody left at the gate. After another five minutes, the ground staff came back, apologised, and said there were two staff members from another gate coming to take me. I had already been waiting for 40 minutes, so I was a little unimpressed.

Eventually, the two staff members did arrive. They were very polite and apologetic over how long I had waited, and they let me know they were very understaffed and that there should have been more people rostered on at the time. Interestingly, they also encouraged me to complain about the treatment I had received because that would help them as well.

We eventually got to the luggage area, and we found my wheelchair. I managed to get to my car OK, but I had been in Melbourne for over two hours by then, which was not acceptable.

I did complain, using the airline's feedback link on their website. A couple of days later, I received a phone call from the Australian manager of client services, who let me know my complaint had been received and verified and that my experience had been poor and completely unacceptable. He then asked me how many were in my family and that he would provide return tickets for all of us to any destination in Australia as a way of making up for the atrocious service I had received. This was not what I expected, but I was grateful, and so the four of us went to Darwin for a few days. On a side note, this was the last capital city in Australia we had not taken the kids to, so we ticked that off that list as well.

A couple of years earlier, the four of us were travelling around the United Kingdom and were scheduled to fly from Edinburgh to London and then on to Paris. By chance, we were watching a local TV news program and discovered British Airways was experiencing some industrial action, and our flights had been cancelled.

We were booked into a place in Paris, and we had a car picking us up at the airport, but now we were not flying.

After heading into an Internet café, we rebooked on EasyJet and then started hearing about all the horror trips and rules that had to be complied with on the low-cost airline. We were a bit apprehensive, but once we got to the terminal, all was good. By now, I was very reliant on the walking stick, and so when we checked into the flight, we were told, because I had some mobility issues, we would get to board first and pick the seats we needed near the front of the plane. This was good news for us, but it was not well received by those passengers who had paid extra to board first and get their pick of the seats. There were several grumpy comments from people who were asking why disabled people and kids got to go on first when they had paid extra for the privilege. It was funny that despite the questions and obvious irritation, they were ignored by everyone, including the aircrew.

A bonus of the change in flight was we flew direct from Edinburgh to Paris instead of changing planes in London. After getting off the plane and collecting our luggage, we needed to go through customs, but as we walked down the aisle towards the security gates, we were beckoned at by a customs officer to come through a special doorway. Because I was using the walking stick and obviously having difficulty walking the distance, we were able to avoid the long wait in the general queue and joined the flight crew through the express lane. We did all the appropriate checking and security stuff, had the passports stamped, and were sent through to the exit to continue our holiday.

Sonja and I travelled to Alaska a few months before the pandemic hit, and the flight was wonderful. For this trip, we had splurged on ourselves and booked premium economy on Air New Zealand, and this turned out to be a very smart thing to do. The seats were brilliant, and the service, drinks, and meals were excellent. It is a long-haul flight, and after partaking of several of the offered drinks, I, of course, needed to use the bathroom. As advised by the cabin crew when we boarded, I pressed the call button, and one of the flight crew came to me. I let him know I needed the bathroom, and he said no problem. He went and got the aisle wheelchair and proceeded to push me to the back of the plane, where there was an accessible toilet. When finished, he then pushed me back to my seat. I was very impressed because despite having flown frequently, I had never experienced a plane with an accessible toilet.

It is wonderful to see airlines and aircraft manufacturers are starting to accommodate disability in their designs. Any flight of more than a couple of hours can be somewhat nerve-wracking for a wheelchair user. Not all aircraft have an aisle chair on board during the flight, so getting to and from the toilet is not possible, and there are not many alternatives.

Chapter 10

The kindness of strangers

I am frequently heartened by the reactions I have received from people who offer to assist me. I often get asked by strangers if they can help in any way. This reinforces the fact that fundamentally people are caring and willing to help others.

I was recently getting into my car after a medical appointment, and a lady who had just parked her car approached and asked if she could assist me. I did not need help but thanked her for the offer.

Several times, when I have been in the city where it is quite hilly, I have been approached by people asking if they can help me up the hill. The request has often been worded as "Please let me help you."

I am grateful when this occurs because having help pushing up a hill is a big benefit to me, and having it offered can be a relief.

A more unconscious assistance I have received is where someone holds the door for me. This can be a door to another room, a lift door, or a door into a building. This occurs frequently and again is welcome.

At other times, I have been invited to a meeting with people, but access for the wheelchair is not available. Once I mention this, the meetings have been moved to places where I can get to, or they have been rescheduled to occur online using technology.

At one point, we were at a wildlife reserve and negotiating some accessible but slightly rugged tracks. I was using the FreeWheel and at one point, was moving slowly down a gentle slope, which had a couple of tree roots across the track. I got over the first one OK, but the second one was at a different angle, and I was tipped out of the wheelchair along with everything else in and under it. I did lose skin from a few areas but also landed on my hip, which stayed unhappy for a few days.

There was the usual panic from everyone, including me, but luckily, a couple of guys who were also visiting the reserve were following us. They turned the corner and saw me on the ground with my wheelchair on its side next to me and ran up to see if they could help. We suggested, if they could lift me back into the wheelchair, that would be a big help, so one of them wrapped his arm around me and put me back in the chair. They asked if we were all OK, which I was, and then we all headed off. If they had not come along when they did, I could have been sitting on the track for quite a while because no one in our group would have been able to lift me as they did.

A very good and appreciated aspect of this was they asked what they could do to help and acted accordingly. It is worth noting that no matter how well intentioned the actions of someone assisting in these situations, it is essential to ask how you can help.

There have been a few occasions when someone has come up behind me and started pushing me without asking or letting me know first. I am normally polite because the intention is well meaning, but I do let them know with a "thank you, but . . .," and they stop.

I seldom get angry or upset with this, but on occasion, I do, especially when the person should know better. I had one instance where I was in a medical facility, getting a Covid inoculation and was following the sign to the exit. One of the nursing staff grabbed the back of my wheelchair and turned me around and started pushing me in the other direction. I stopped the chair, and she told me I could not use that exit because it had stairs and that I needed to go back the way I had come to use the lift. I let her know I would push myself and that I did not need her to push the chair for me and that I did not appreciate being manhandled without at least letting me know why.

Her response made it obvious that she did not understand why I was not appreciative of her efforts.

In the same facility, I was offered assistance by several staff who asked if there was anything they could do for me. This was appropriate, although not needed, but appreciated.

Chapter 11

Tourist destinations and disability

Over the years, we have travelled to some fascinating places around the world. Most of them have been visited since I was diagnosed with HSP. This has seen me travel using the walking stick initially, but for the past ten years, I have travelled with the wheelchair. Many of the places we have been to quite unexpectedly provided very good access for wheelchair users, whereas others that I would expect to be OK have actually been less than adequate.

New Zealand is one place I have travelled extensively through, partially because I lived there for 20 years, from the time I was ten, but also because I would often travel back to visit family and friends. The touristy areas I have travelled in, particularly in the last ten years, have been relatively accommodating to a wheelchair user.

Like many Western cities around the world, there are sites or venues easily accessible in a wheelchair; however, the older the building, generally, the less wheelchair-friendly they are. Where possible and required by law, owners or occupiers have tried their best to adapt to a changing world and installed ramps or elevators; however, this isn't always possible, so sometimes I just have to accept I am not getting into that restaurant or that venue.

Parks and gardens, of course, are generally accessible, so long as they don't have one of those turnstile entrances that were so popular in the 1950s to keep the riff-raff out. Unless the town has had a lot of rain, my FreeWheel allows me to traverse the often gravel walkways with relative ease.

Over the years, we have spent time in Christchurch, Ashburton, Queenstown, and have also travelled along the West Coast as far south as Franz Joseph and through the Haast Pass into Wanaka and Queenstown. We have also travelled up the East Coast from Dunedin through to Kaikoura, Blenheim, and the Marlborough Sounds.

Most places we stayed at were able to accommodate the wheelchair, but at the time, I was still able to walk a little and climb a step or two. I was also travelling with Sonja, who could assist me as needed.

New Zealand is well known for its coastline, mountains, lakes, and scenery. There are many walking and hiking tracks, most of which are appropriate for the experienced tramper, hiker, with the right equipment. The majority of these tracks are, of course, unsuitable for wheelchairs because they are steep, rugged, and often narrow. There are a few that are OK for wheelchairs, but if you ever decide to travel on them, they will need to be checked before venturing onto them because conditions often change, mostly because of the weather. Despite this, there are still many places to stop along the road and revel in the landscapes without having to go too far off the beaten track.

We have been fortunate to have travelled overseas a few times over the past 13 or so years. Initially, I was using the walking stick but have been using the wheelchair for the last ten years.

Since being fully wheelchair-bound, we have undertaken a couple of cruises in the Baltic and Alaska. Our experience on these ships has been excellent, with many benefits for a person using a wheelchair. Once you have boarded the ship, one of the main benefits is you only have to unpack once, yet you get to see so many fabulous cities and vistas. Being wheelchair-bound means the "tour bus" way of travelling is extra taxing. You have to get on and off the bus—that is, assuming they have a wheelchair lift on the bus—then you have to unpack and repack at every overnight stop. The bus often leaves early in the morning, and as I have already said, I am not a fast dresser. I could see me being left behind very quickly on a traditional tour-bus trip.

On the cruise, however, I get to decide my pace of life. If I don't want to get up early to whiz off to the next shore excursion, I don't have to. I can plan my day at my pace yet still see the things I want to see.

We learned early on it is necessary to book an accessible cabin early. Happily, we have also been questioned each time we booked an accessible cabin so the cruise line can ascertain if we really need the facilities. While some people might be offended by the inference, I appreciate the efforts the companies put in to ensure these precious few cabins are only sold to those who really need them and who would not be able to participate in the cruise without these facilities.

The cabins on the ships we have booked have had the appropriate shower and toilet for a wheelchair user as well as often having a closet that allows you to pull down the hanging rail so I can reach my clothes from my chair. Also, the rooms are slightly bigger, which is why they are so popular with other cruisers, which allows me to maneuver my wheelchair relatively easily.

Many areas of the ship are accessible, and I haven't come across a single restaurant yet that I haven't been able to access. There was, however, one bar on a ship that was on the top mezzanine deck and only had stair access. There were plenty of other bars on the ship, though, so I didn't miss out on making the most use of my beverage package.

Fortunately, most decks on the ship also have accessible toilets—a major necessity when utilising said beverage package!

The part of the ship that can be most difficult in a wheelchair is the carpet used in the corridors and many of the common areas. Carpet definitely makes pushing the wheelchair a bit more of an effort. I, however, have been fortunate to have Sonja with me. She is always willing to push me wherever I am having difficulty. This is based on her theory that if she works off a few calories pushing me around, she can then indulge in desserts or cocktails as a reward. If she has overindulged, I tend to get pushed around a lot.

The last cruise we took was to Alaska, and we organised all the shore excursions via the cruise line so our accessibility needs would be understood. For the most part, this worked, and there was only one room on the overland part of the tour that caused a minor inconvenience.

The landscape of Alaska is absolutely beautiful, and great effort has gone into making as much of it as accessible as possible. Buses and trains all seem to have lifts or ramps to get the wheelchairs on and off, and staff have been trained on using the equipment.

In Alaska, it was essential to have the FreeWheel with us so I could get around the towns and nature tracks and to also get to the water's edge to see waterfalls and the views from off the road. The beauty of Alaska is it is still relatively untamed. Remember Joni Michell singing, "They paved paradise, put up a parking lot." I would certainly not wish to see that enabling me to see glaciers and waterfalls is provided by paving over and smoothing out the natural environment.

In truth, I was able to see all that I wanted to see by using the FreeWheel and the access available. The HSP means there are places I cannot get to because of my physical limitations, and I am fine with that.

When travelling in Europe, accessibility, particularly for wheelchairs, is still very good, remembering that many of the buildings were constructed hundreds of years ago.

Many of the older buildings have had some minor modifications so a wheelchair can get inside, although upper levels may not be reachable. We were lucky enough to have had a private tour of the Aachen Dom (cathedral) arranged by Sonja's cousin. I was able to reach almost all of the Dom and saw where Charlemagne was buried and the various areas of the cathedral. The only part of the tour I wasn't able to participate in was special access to the belfry and roof area, where Sonja and the kids had an almost 360-degree view of the city.

Europe has many ancient buildings and a great number of old buildings. The ancient buildings include those that predate the Roman occupation, such as Stonehenge, the many barrows in France, Spain, and United Kingdom. There are also a great number of buildings that date back to Roman times; some of which are still in use.

The buildings that date back to the Middle Ages include many churches and cathedrals, houses, and the innumerable castles evident across Europe.

When we were in England, we visited a few castles still in use for either military or ceremonial purposes. We went to the Tower of London, Edinburgh Castle, and also Carlisle Castle. I was using the walking stick because I did not need the wheelchair at the time. There were some parts of these castles I could not get to, but I was able to get around most of them.

The Tower of London was fascinating for many reasons but mostly for its age; it is still in use today as a garrison for the Yeomen Warders and is where the crown jewels are kept. It is also a museum for the preservation of the buildings and displaying medieval clothing, weaponry, and armour. Although I was using the walking stick, because of fatigue, I was unable to get to some of the areas accessed by flights of stairs. It would have been good to have had the use of a wheelchair for some of this, but at the time I was not ready to accept the inevitable.

Similarly, in Edinburgh, we went to a castle that is very well preserved and still in use, but this also involved a lot of walking. Most of the roads and pedestrian areas are cobbled, which makes it tiring and interesting to walk around.

The castle itself is interesting not only in its history but also as a working castle that still has a military garrison on the grounds. I have learned, since we were there, there has been a significant updating of facilities to accommodate people with disabilities.

Below the castle is the Royal Mile, which is home to a number of tourist shops. We spent time wandering around these shops and dissuading the kids from buying swords and armour. The Royal Mile is also cobbled, which made walking around a little precarious at times. The stick can get stuck between the cobbles, and because there is a slight incline, it requires concentration to ensure a fall-free stroll.

We had signed up for a ghost tour in the evening. It was well done, and the stories were interesting and macabre. Using the walking stick in the dark was an experience because the ground cannot be seen, so I never knew what I was putting the stick onto, and you can't tell when the stick is caught between the cobbles until you find it doesn't move when you pull on it. We had a great time in Edinburgh and enjoyed it tremendously, although I did get very tired with the amount of walking needed.

After Edinburgh, we travelled to Paris, where we had some interesting experiences, which again highlighted the goodwill people generally have for others. We only had a few days there and wanted to see some of the uniquely Parisian sites, such as the Eiffel Tower, Notre Dame Cathedral, and the Louvre. This was before I needed the wheelchair but was very dependent on my walking stick.

As you may already know, the Eiffel Tower has lifts that take you to the two viewing platforms, or the cheaper option is to walk up the stairs. There was no way I would have been able to walk up the two flights of stairs, so we decided we would definitely splurge on the elevator. Everywhere else we were going on this trip to Europe, we had prebooked; however, there was a small note on the website that stated if you couldn't walk down the stairs in an emergency, they would not allow you up the elevator. Rather than risk wasting our tourist dollars on a ticket I could not use, we decided to take a gamble and buy our tickets on site. We discovered the queues are massive, and it ended up being a three-hour wait before we could buy our tickets to go up the tower. In the end, nobody queried my ability to walk back down. Next time, we'll ignore the fine print and prebook.

While in Paris, we couldn't leave without at least a quick look through the Louvre. When we got there, it was later on a very busy day, and I was tired from walking everywhere. As we walked through the foyer, a gentleman approached me and asked me, in English, if I would like a wheelchair. At that point, I could have kissed him. It was many years later that I learned my acceptance of the wheelchair was a big surprise for my daughter who had expected me to refuse it and continue walking. I think this was when she discovered my abilities were deteriorating more than a little.

With Sonja pushing me in the wheelchair, we set off to visit a few of the exhibits. As our time was limited, we had to pick and choose what we would see. First off, of course, was the *Mona Lisa*. The Louvre is a wonderful museum never built with wheelchair users in mind. Even with a map, we were unable to navigate the various lifts and half floors or mezzanine levels we had to negotiate to get to the correct level.

We approached one of the guards and explained where we wanted to go and asked for directions. The response was a smile and "follow me." He led us to a wall, where he entered a code into a keypad, and a part of the wall slid back to reveal a gap between the walls. Once inside, the wall behind us closed, and the wall in front opened, and we were where we wanted to be. I am quite sure we would not have been taken "through the wall" had I not been using the wheelchair. Once we got to the *Mona Lisa*, Sonja and I were ushered in front of the security rope, in front of the crowd of visitors, giving us an uninterrupted view of the painting. The kids were stuck at the back of the crowd with everyone else.

My mobility continued to decline, and while I could walk a couple of steps when we were in Europe, it quite quickly progressed to where I could no longer go anywhere without using the wheelchair. In 2016, we were in Germany, and we visited a town called Monschau, which has a castle built on a hill overlooking the town. This castle is used for a number of purposes nowadays, and when we were there, they were luckily hosting a couple of bands we wanted to see.

Getting to the castle requires a trip up a steep and winding road, which gets you to the main gate. There is then another steep and cobbled road you need to walk up, which takes you from the main gate to the castle proper, where the band performs.

The organisers did a magnificent job of putting these functions on, and I was advised I would be looked after when attending the concert. You cannot take a car to the castle, but buses had been arranged to get you up to the main gate. Each bus has a fold-down ramp to enable wheelchairs to get onto the bus and dedicated positions for up to two wheelchairs once inside the bus.

When we got off the bus at the main gate, we were met by the Red Cross, who took care of all those with disabilities. They had volunteers who pushed me up the steep cobbled road to where the stage was set up. Once there, a platform had been built specifically near the front for those in wheelchairs and their carers or partners to watch the band from. At least one chair was set up for each spot so the person in the wheelchair could enjoy the band with at least one friend or carer. All the other seating were on tiers, accessed by steps, so not for disabled people. During the concert, if I needed to use the toilet, I only needed to signal the Red Cross volunteer who would wheel me to the accessible toilet and return me to the viewing platform afterwards.

When the concert ended, we got back to our cars the same way we got up to the castle but in reverse, including being taken from the platform back down the steep and cobbled road to the main gate by the Red Cross team. It was all very efficient and simple and highly organised.

In most places around Europe, the footpaths are quite OK for a wheelchair, and most intersections have the usual lowered kerb that will accommodate prams, wheelchairs, and similar. The exception to this was Saint Petersburg, which could be difficult without assistance in getting over the kerbs.

Saint Petersburg is a very beautiful city, and all the places we visited were as part of a tour group, which is a condition of the visa we were granted. When booking the two-day tour, we had advised the tour company about my mobility issues. At the time of visiting this part of Russia, I was using the wheelchair, but I was able to walk a few steps using a walking stick; however, I was also capable of climbing up to four stairs. As is often the case, even though we had sent a number of e-mails detailing what I could and couldn't do, we found the tour leader had not been made aware of my mobility limitations. As such, at each venue we visited, she had to confer with the on-site staff about what accommodations could be made for me. In one or two places, I had to leave the group and be escorted by a staff member to an elevator and meet up with the group on the next level or room, depending on the venue.

For example, the Faberge Museum was accessible; however, I was separated from the group and taken up a service elevator, while the rest of the tour group climbed the stairs to the next level. It was a little daunting to be whisked away by total strangers, with whom I couldn't communicate as none of them spoke English and I don't speak Russian. Nonetheless, I was quickly reunited with Sonja and the group, and we all enjoyed the exhibition.

We were lucky to be able to visit the Summer Palace and its gardens. This was a truly beautiful place, and I can just imagine how it must have looked when it first opened. In the palace, the lifts have been ingeniously installed away from the main areas of the buildings but do provide access to all areas. Here, again, I was separated from the group, but this time Sonja was able to go with me as a staff member took us to the lifts and up to the correct floor to join the group. It was necessary for the staff member to stay with us so we could be taken back down the lifts to join the rest of our group outside.

As I have mentioned, we enjoy being outside and seeing the natural environment, and while this can be difficult in a wheelchair, there are some places where the needs of disabled people have been considered in the design of the attractions.

We spent time at the Nationalpark Eifel in Germany. This park is a rehabilitated part of the Eifel, which is being restored to its natural state. All introduced trees and plants are or have been removed, and only plants indigenous to the area are being replanted. Once the initial replanting is done, no further interference is undertaken. The forest is simply allowed to grow and flourish as nature intended. As part of the rehabilitation effort, a lot of thought has gone into ensuring the pathways and signage are suitable for people with a variety of disabilities. Not only have the tracks been leveled for easy wheelchair and pram access, but there are also several sensory sections along the walks, where vision-impaired people can experience the sounds of the park with information available in Braille. Those with hearing loss are also provided with many visual displays along the path, with pictures and explanations in several languages.

On another trip to Germany, we visited Berlin, which is a vibrant and exciting city. We saw many of the usual tourist spots, such as the Brandenburg Gate and Checkpoint Charlie, but one of the most interesting was the Reichstag. This building has been the seat of the German government since 1999. We prebooked our tickets to visit the site two months in advance, and the visit included a tour of the building and access to the Kuppel, which is the glass dome at the top of the building. As you would expect, security into the Reichstag is very tight, and we needed to go through a security screening to gain access; however, once inside, we were escorted around as part of an allocated tour. After an English-speaking tour of the main parts of the building, we got to the Kuppel by using a lift to get to the right level. At this point, we were handed audio headphones and devices so we could make our way up the sloping ramp at our pace. The slope of the ramp was so gentle that it allowed me to push myself up at my pace while listening to the audio information of the various sights that could be seen. Not being forced to travel at someone else's pace is a luxury I don't often get.

As with domestic holidays in Australia, near and far, it is always necessary to plan ahead to find out what sort of facilities would be available. What you require will be personal, depending on your needs; however, I am generally still able to transfer myself, even if steps are no longer possible. Once transferring becomes an issue, we will need to be more selective in our holiday destinations; however, I have heard you can hire hoists and the like in many different places, and lots of hotels and tourist sites have contact details for local hiring companies.

There is one thing I am certain of: My wheelchair will not stop me from going out and experiencing new things and seeing the wonders of this world.

Have wheelchair, will travel!

Chapter 12

Advice for travelling

Whether you are going on an overnight trip in your local town or an extended overseas holiday, it is necessary to prepare. Ultimately, you know what you will need to make your travels easier and hassle free, but there are some things that can be done to help you do this.

I have put some things down here, which have assisted me immensely with my travels, and these may assist you as well.

- Plan.
    - o Where are you going?
    - o How are you getting there?
    - o What facilities are available?
    - o What may be a problem there?
    - o How can these problems be overcome or managed?
    - o Travel Insurance is an essential item.
- Know your capabilities.
    - o What can I do?
    - o What can I perhaps be OK with?
    - o What can I not do?
    - o What can I do if assisted by
        - A complete stranger?
        - A carer?
        - A partner?

- Contact the property and asking about their facilities.
    - o It is wise to contact the places where you will be staying and identifying what may be in place to meet your needs, but you also need to be prepared for the answer to be misleading. We often ask for a photo to be sent to us so we can see what the facilities actually are. You will often have a reassuring voice tell you the room is designed for a wheelchair user and the bathroom has rails and a wheel-in shower, but when you arrive, the description does not match your expectations. A photograph will help give you an idea of what is actually available for you.
- Do not assume anything.
    - o Even if you have been told accessible facilities are available, be prepared that they may not be as described or even there at all. Ask for a photo. As an example, I was invited out for lunch at a wedding reception venue with a large group of people. As I always do now, I called the venue and asked about wheelchair access to the building and also about accessible toilets. I was advised there were a couple of steps to get into the building, but there was a ramp they can set up for me. They also said they had an accessible toilet. When I arrived, I needed to ask another guest to find a staff member who can set up the ramp for me. This was fine, and I got into the room OK. The tables for lunch, however, were too close together so I was very limited in where I could sit. I, of course, needed to use the toilet but could not find it because there was only a gents and a ladies. I couldn't get into the gents because the door was too narrow, so I had to ask a staff member where the accessible toilet was. She did not know, so she had to ask her manager. It turned out they did not have an accessible toilet at all, but they did have a cubicle in the ladies' toilet that was bigger than the others, and I could use that. There was a handrail, but the cubicle was definitely not

accessible, although with some fiddling, I did manage to get my wheelchair close enough to transfer onto the toilet. There were some very surprised faces when a man emerged from the loo and into where the ladies were busy chatting and touching up their makeup. This is an example of how despite doing all the right things about finding out if your needs can be accommodated, the information provided makes it sound as though you will be OK when, in fact, you will not be.

- Have a contingency.
  - o There are some items you will need with you but which you may not use. For a wheelchair, one of the risks is damage. I carry spare inner tubes, tools for removing tyres, and a pump with me when I travel so if I do get a puncture, I can repair it without having to find a bike shop.
  - o I also carry a set of Allen keys with me for when bits come loose or need adjusting.
  - o I also carry gloves with me and use them when out to protect my hands from injury. I have caught my fingers in the brake and occasionally on the hand rim, which hurts and can be quite serious, depending on where you are. Band-Aids are a necessary item to have with you.
- Be prepared to complain.
  - o A complaint can often resolve the problem, but if not, then you may get some assistance to find an alternative.
- Identify what you will need with you.
  - o Take what you need with you if you have it.
  - o Purchase what you will need before you go, if you can.
  - o Where can you purchase or hire what you need at your destination?
  - o What medications do I need to have with me?
    - Do they need special storage?
    - Are they legal where you are going? Many medications legal in Australia are illegal, restricted, or unavailable elsewhere.

- Do you have enough for the whole trip? You may have difficulty getting the same medication in another country.
- Do you need a doctor's letter to explain the medications? It is far better to have this and not need it than to need it and not have it.

- Do your research so you know what to expect, but prepare for what may happen that was not expected. This may be as described earlier, where the shower is over a bath and getting to it is difficult, or where the seat is at one end of the shower but the taps are at the other end and unreachable. Worst case is where the facilities cannot accommodate your needs at all, in which case knowing what you can and can't do is important in planning how to get around the problem.
- Remember, other people may talk about accessibility and what people in wheelchairs need, but in reality, they do not know, so even if you are told the bathroom is wheelchair-friendly, it may not be.
- Travel insurance is essential when travelling for many obvious reasons, especially so for people with disabilities, but some are not so obvious.
  o Lost luggage, damage, missed connections, and similar can be addressed through the travel insurance.
  o Illness or injury caused by accident, falling, etc, which may require medical assistance or hospitalisation, can be covered by travel insurance.
  o It will also pay to let the travel insurance provider know what your condition is and identifying what you may need and is available with the travel cover and understanding any exclusions.
  o Understand that travel insurance is something you need but do not expect to use. It is there to help with managing the unexpected, and unfortunately, the unexpected happens more frequently with us disabled people.

Chapter 13

Working and social life with a Disability

As previously mentioned, I started showing very mild symptoms of HSP when I was about 48 years old, manifesting as the occasional catching of my toes, foot drop, when walking. Mainly it was my right foot that caught the edge of paving stones, kerbs, or any slight rough patch on the footpath. This went on for several months before my colleagues started to mention it to me. I had noticed it myself but put it down to uneven footpaths, bluestone kerbs, and similar.

Back when I turned 40, my work colleagues transformed my office at work and for a joke, had given me a walking stick, which was funny at the time and ended up in a cupboard at home.

I decided I should start using the walking stick because I had stumbled a few times and had had a few falls where I had caught my toe and embraced the footpath. This had caused me to feel a little less than secure when walking. The walking stick provided me with some confidence, but it was a long way from what I needed. It was very thin and also too short for me; however, at the time, it met the need and saved me from falling several times.

After a while, I came to the realisation the walking stick I was using was not strong or tall enough for me to continue using it. I, therefore, purchased a taller and more substantial walking stick, which I could use to lean on. This was much better and provided a much-needed support.

Over time I became very reliant on the stick and because I was quite unsteady, did not take a step without it.

I started going to a physiotherapy group that specialised in neurological conditions. After my initial assessment and the first couple of sessions, I was advised the walking stick I was using was too short for me and that I needed a walking stick more suited to my height. Using the advice, I purchased another walking stick that met the criteria. Once I started using the new stick, I found I was standing more upright and that my posture when walking was more comfortable.

About two years after my diagnosis, I changed jobs and went to work for a company that provided IT systems to communities of aged and disability organisations. I was using the walking stick at my interview, and when I started working there, the walking stick was part of my work outfit: suit, tie, shiny shoes, walking stick. I momentarily thought I needed to match my shoes to the walking stick but then decided it was all too silly, so black shoes, brown stick just had to work.

This was my first role where most of my colleagues had never known me without my disability; everybody saw the stick, but very few of my new colleagues commented on it. I never felt my use of a walking stick had any detrimental impact on how my workmates saw me or how I performed my role.

Over time my walking became more difficult, but I persisted with the stick. I just got slower. I also found my shoulder became sore because I was putting a lot of weight on it when walking.

I drove to work, and the parking outside the office was for three hours, but because by this stage, I had qualified for a disability tag for the car, I got double the time, so I had six hours of parking. Unfortunately, I worked an eight-hour day, so after a while, I started getting parking tickets. I ended up with three $80 tickets in a week, which was not expected. My employer was equally upset and offered me a car park on the premises, which was appreciated and very welcome. All other staff parked in a car park just up the road, but this was too far for me to walk to and from.

The area of the organisation I worked in was acquired by a very large telecommunications company, and we moved to another floor of the building. At that point, my walking using the stick had become more precarious, and I had fallen a couple of times, so I decided to stop being stubborn and started to use a wheelchair. This was a major move for me.

When I first went into the office in the wheelchair, many of my colleagues came to see me and have a look at the new device. Almost everyone made the comment that it was about bloody time! My confidence was restored, and from that point on, I was mobile again.

I did notice I was suddenly a short person. Having been a touch over 6 feet tall, 183 centimetres, when I could walk, viewing the world from about 4 feet 6 inches was very different. I found I had to look up to everyone, even the short people, which was quite amusing for a while. Then I discovered looking up to everyone gave me a sore neck.

I was fortunate to work for a company that was understanding and supportive of my mobility limitations. They installed an accessible toilet, which was very welcome. They even purchased an evacuation chair for me to use if there was a fire in the building. This was a chair that was able to roll over the stairs without having to bump down step by step. It did require someone to control the descent and to steer it as needed while I sat in the seat and did nothing but remain calm. In some respects, I became cargo being moved in a sack barrow.

We did a couple of practice runs with this, which was interesting and without the pressure of smoke and flames, was quite enjoyable. Once we knew it worked OK, I was always advised in advance of any evacuation drills so I could be out of the building before they started.

As with all employment, I decided to apply for a role in another part of the business, for which I was interviewed and was successful. I took up a role in the hospital division, which meant I moved from the city fringe to a larger office in the Melbourne CBD.

Being in a multistory CBD building, fire drills and evacuation processes were a requirement. Because of my need for a wheelchair, I was unable to become a fire warden, so I became a fire warden's problem.

I totally adopted this role and endeavoured to live up to the expectations this position engendered. It never became a problem until the first fire drill. The alarms went off, and we had to evacuate the building. The fire wardens were running around like sheepdogs at a muster, but people are not sheep and did not respond well when being pushed to evacuate the building. I grew up in New Zealand, and I know sheep are a lot easier to work with. There are no arguments, no gathering up of personal items and stuff, they don't ring other people to tell them there is a fire alarm and that the building must be evacuated. Oh, and by the way, I may be late home for dinner tonight because of this fire alarm, and how did child A go with the assignment? Did we get good marks? How's the dog? Did you talk to the neighbours? I need to get the car serviced. The train was late. Lunch was pretty average. Oh sorry, gotta go, they are evacuating the building. You get the idea!

I, on the other hand, head for the exit immediately and am confronted with the sign "in the event of a fire, do not use the lift." OK, this is a fire, so I won't use the lift. Oh no, the evac chair did not follow me to the new office; it is still at the old office. What do I do now? Easy, ask the fire warden who knows all about this stuff.

There he is. "Hey, fire warden, I can't use the lift because there is a fire. How do I evacuate the building?"

At this point, you realise the fire warden had not considered how to get the wheelchair guy down the stairs. The response was, "Hang on here, and I will find out," and I watched the FW run away.

Eventually, he came back and explained how I was going to evacuate the building. It is really quite simple. I go to the service lift foyer, which is behind some smoke-proof doors and wait. I will be quite safe there because the fire and smoke will never get to where I am because there is a smoke-proof and fire-resistant door between me and the inferno.

It's not that I doubted the advice, but the doors I was looking at seemed to be made of aluminium foil reinforced with cardboard. I may have been mistaken, but that was my impression.

And then what? Well, I wait in front of the lifts in the safe area, which is fire- and smoke-resistant, and the fire brigade will rescue me. In other words, please stay inside the burning building, and if someone, possibly a fire warden, remembers to advise the fire brigade that there is a guy in a wheelchair waiting to be rescued, I may survive the fire.

Let's just say I was a little unconvinced.

After the evacuation drill, I raised my concerns and advised the company about the evac chair, which they said they would get.

Having moved into the hospital division, I found myself working with a number of others with whom I had worked in the past. It was good to get reacquainted with them after several years, and it was amazing how much and how little had changed.

Getting back into the hospital space after a number of years away was good but also a little disappointing because there did not seem to be much by way of improvement to the systems being used in the hospitals nor any significant change to processes. Many of the limitations of technology with the hospital sector were still there, and although a lot of the technology could accommodate the needed changes, the hospitals themselves were very slow to identify and adopt the technology.

My role required me to visit the hospitals and meet with senior executive staff and IT staff. Mostly this was quite straightforward, and because these are hospitals, accessibility for a wheelchair user was no issue. Occasionally, however, when meeting at the corporate office, which was not within a hospital, accessibility was not as simple.

One of my clients was a large hospital group, and I needed to attend a meeting with the CEO of the private hospitals in their corporate office. My manager and I attended together, and once we had arrived, we were faced with a flight of steps up to the front door.

This is where the fun started. At the side of the steps was a hoist for wheelchairs, which is a flip-down platform you can put the wheelchair onto; it then puts safety rails up so you can't roll off. It then moves up the steps and deposits you at the top. Once there, the safety rails come down so you can roll off the platform and into the building. Very simple.

However, the steps are on a public street next to the footpath, and because the hospital group do not want anybody coming along and playing with the wheelchair hoist, it is locked. There is also an intercom arrangement, so when you need the hoist, you press the intercom, speak to whoever responds, who will then come out with the key, and get you up and going.

Only issue is someone needs to answer the intercom. When that does not occur, there is a phone number to call, but that is provided on a piece of paper stuck on a window at the top of the steps. So to see the phone number, you need to use the hoist to get to the top of the steps, so you can call the number, so someone can make the hoist available. You may notice a problem with this.

Fortunately, my manager was able to climb the steps and call the number attached to the window. The call was answered, and as the person knew nothing about the wheelchair hoist, they offered to find someone who did. This duly happened, and after about 20 minutes, a delightful young man came out with the key. This was a new experience for all of us because he had never used the device and had no idea of what to do. I had used similar devices, and together, we explored how best to make it work.

The key was inserted and turned, and lights appeared on the control panel. I then rolled onto the platform from the back because only one of the safety rails had opened, so I was facing the street rather than where I was going. No problem. We then got the platform moving, and it slowly climbed towards the top of the steps.

Once we got there, it stopped, the safety rail moved out of the way, and the platform flipped up into the parked position. The only problem was I was still on the platform at the time. The result of this was I and my wheelchair were flipped off the platform backwards, where the wheelchair landed on its back. I fell out and hit the wall of the building, and everyone around me had conniptions to varying degrees.

Although I had banged my head on the wall, I thought the whole episode was funny. Basically, it took about half an hour to get up the steps, and once at the top, I was thrown off.

We finally got inside the building and used the elevator to get to the executive level for our meeting. The exec in question had been apprised of the problem with the wheelchair lift and that I had hit my head on the wall. His comment to me was he hoped I was OK and it was lucky I had hit my head only and not something important. This is executive-level humour.

We finished the meeting, and we ventured forth on the return expedition. It was decided we should not risk the wheelchair hoist again, and instead, we descended into the car park and used the ramp to get me back to street level and back to the office. My poor manager then had to write an incident report about what happened and register the fact that I had hit my head. Following this, I had several calls from HR to ask if I was alright and that I was not hurt or having any trauma as a result. Although the concern was welcome, I still found the whole episode amusing. I may have felt differently if there had been significant damage to me or my wheelchair, but as this was not the case, I found the whole experience quite funny. I found out afterwards the hospital group also had to put an incident report in. I never did find out if the wheelchair hoist was ever repaired.

I was working as an account manager and reporting to the sales manager, and we had sales planning meetings annually. I attended one of these in Sydney over two days and as well as meeting colleagues from the other states; there were some guests invited to give talks on their experiences, which would provide incentive and perspective on our roles.

The guest at this planning session, a friend of the sales manager, was an ultra-marathon athlete and had been blind since birth. His talk was fascinating, and his achievements would have been totally awesome if an able-bodied person had done them, but as a blind person, the achievements and experiences are simply mindboggling. His talk described his training regimen and preparations for his running. He has run from Cairns to Brisbane five times. Because of his inability to see when he runs, he needs a running partner with him, who guides him using a tether, which links his wrist with the companion runner's wrist.

He told us about his friends who run with him but also like playing jokes on him. They have run him into swimming pools for a laugh as well as other things. I have mentioned this to other people who have been shocked and upset that anyone would do this to a vision-impaired person and see it as quite wrong. My initial reaction was similar, but after listening to him for a while longer, it became obvious he had a sense of humour; he was not upset by it and saw it for the joke that it was, even though it was at his expense.

In a lot of respects, this shows, despite what other people see as a debilitating affliction, the person who is managing it does not necessarily think of it in that way. In fact, the joke and pranks are welcome because they occur between people who are friends and who are seen as peers and not as someone who has to be tiptoed around or treated differently.

Funnily enough, there was an excursion provided on the last day, and we were all taken to the wharf, where a series of jet boats were waiting to take us on a trip around Sydney Harbour. I was, of course, in my wheelchair and could not get onto the boats, so I waved goodbye to them as they sped off in a spray of saltwater then went back to the bar and waited for them to return.

Although I am sure I was not purposely excluded from this part of the session, my needs had not been considered or catered for, which was disappointing. I was not really surprised by this because out of approximately 80 people, I was the only one who used a wheelchair, and when planning events, the majority are the focus for consideration.

I was working there for about another year when a downsizing exercise was initiated, and along with a number of others, I was retrenched. I had a few months off, and then I successfully applied for a role with another health IT provider, and the fact that I used a wheelchair was not a consideration or a problem.

There was only ever one minor inconvenience for me with my last office-based role, that the accessible toilet was on a different floor, not a major problem unless there was an urgency to use the facility, which fortunately never occurred.

We were set up in a shared office space on the second floor, while the accessible toilet was on the third floor. This meant I needed to get to the lift, press the button, wait for the lift to arrive, enter the lift, use my access dongle to show I was allowed to use the lift, press the third-floor button, exit the lift, wheel down the corridor to the shared tea/coffee-making area, touch the pad to unlock the door, open the door, wheel in to the accessible toilet, hope it was not in use, open the door, wheel in, lock the door, do what had to be done, wash hands, and then do the same thing in reverse to get back to the office.

And people wonder why it takes about half an hour for me to go for a pee!

There was an accessible toilet on the second floor, but it was a female-only toilet. I was told the male toilet also had an accessible cubicle, but it was actually an ambulatory toilet, which does not have room for a wheelchair. This is a common misunderstanding by those who don't use a wheelchair.

You may wonder why I would tell you about accessible toilets. A person who does not need one can safely assume, wherever they are, they can use the options available, so it is not a consideration.

If you do need an accessible toilet, it becomes part of the planning process and is a major consideration. As an example, going out for dinner to a restaurant or a friend's house will at some point require a bladder to be emptied. If there are no places that can accommodate the wheelchair, then the task becomes extremely difficult or impossible. It's not like you can go outside and pee on a tree, so it will require planning and research beforehand.

An interesting part of working in an office environment for a large company is the desire of the company to protect their workforce and to provide motivation to their staff to stay healthy, keep fit, look after their mental health, etc.

A number of things have been put in place to help the staff maintain their health, attitude, well-being, etc, and I must admit to having a little fun with these things. I made it known there was absolutely no way I would participate in a "walking meeting," which many managers used to improve their fitness by meeting staff while going for a walk.

Another thing was to get up and walk around every hour. Again, not something I was going to do. A number of posters were put up in communal areas, which said things like "Get up off your bum/bottom/ tushie and walk around for a few minutes." "Don't use the lift, take the stairs." A number of e-mails would also be sent out to reinforce the message about getting up and going for a walk.

I have been known to derive some amusement by playing the part of an outraged disabled person being humiliated by their able-bodied colleagues. I did say to some of the people with whom I worked that all these signs and e-mails about getting up off your bum and going for a walk made me feel less as a person and humiliated that I could not participate in things that were essential to my well-being and the goals of the company. I mentioned I was starting to feel inadequate and was letting the team down by not getting up for a walk and not using the stairs.

Now most of my colleagues know I am just having some fun, but someone told someone else who told someone else until the fun part was lost and someone raised it with HR that I was unhappy because the signage and expectations were things I could not do and this was having a very detrimental impact on my self-esteem, my ability to work within the team, and my ability to meet the expectations of the company.

Much to my surprise, I had a visit at my desk from a reasonably senior HR manager, who wanted to find out about how I was feeling and if there was anything that needed addressing for my well-being. They were particularly concerned that their efforts to promote activity and well-being for the majority of the workforce was having the opposite effect on me and that I needed to be aware that there were avenues provided by the employer for counselling and physical- and mental-health services I could use, if needed. There was certainly no intention by the company to belittle my physical limitations or to make me feel inadequate or humiliated by their activities for the wider workforce.

This person was very serious and was going to great lengths to make sure I was being included and that these messages and posters were in no way put around to make me feel discriminated against, humiliated, or inadequate and what could HR do to make things easier for me.

In life, every now and then, you have the "oh shit" moment. The HR conversation was one of my "oh shit" moments.

These people were seriously concerned that their actions to help the well-being of the team had, in fact, alienated one of them and was having serious impacts on my mental health and feelings of self-confidence and value to the organisation.

Oh no, what do I do now? What I did was start laughing, which was probably not the correct thing to do, but the milk was spilt now. I explained to the HR person I was being an arse and that I was not offended, humiliated, upset, or suffering from feelings of inadequacy.

I further explained I am a person who has some mobility issues and use a wheelchair, but I work in an environment where I am definitely in the minority and that initiatives put forward by the organisation can only be designed to accommodate the majority of staff. The "get up off your bum" initiative is well worth having and promoting, and I am not adversely affected by it. I added there were plenty of things a person in a wheelchair could get upset about, but these were way outside what HR could do anything about.

I did, however, reiterate the fire escape plan for me was somewhat flawed and that did actually concern me, particularly now that it had been several months since I had raised it and I'd had assurances from HR that there would be action around getting an escape chair for me, but nothing had happened so far.

Anyway, on the one hand, the HR guy was understanding and would follow up about the escape chair but was mildly pissed off I was not too worried about the posters around the place or going for a walk and getting up off my bum.

On a slightly different perspective, many of my work colleagues who knew me a little better thought the whole thing was a joke and my reaction was totally in keeping with the way I am.

It is funny in a tragic sort of way when you check that a restaurant has an accessible toilet before you go and they say they have, but when you get there, you find they actually don't have one, but you can use the staff toilet out the back and no one will look. The other one that makes me laugh out loud is where the accessible toilet is upstairs and there is no lift. It may only be two steps, but for me, it may as well be 100.

Working in an account-management position regularly entailed taking clients out for lunch or dinner. When using a wheelchair, the venue and its facilities are important considerations. As an example of the planning involved, we went out to dinner recently with some friends to a restaurant we had wanted to go to for several years. As I normally do, I contacted the restaurant to ask about accessibility and toilets. The reviews I read said there was wheelchair access, but on enquiring by telephone and e-mail, the responses were slightly different.

When speaking to the restaurant and asking about using a wheelchair, I was advised that yes, the restaurant was accessible. There were steps up to the front door, but they had a ramp they would put down for me.

The e-mail I received also mentioned the ramp but also advised me that "the toilets are accessible, as in I could get into the toilets, but the cubicles are all standard width so not able to accommodate the wheelchair." This, of course, meant, from my perspective, even though the toilets were on the ground floor, they were not accessible; however, the restaurant considered they were. The information provided was accurate and enabled me to go to the restaurant knowing I would be unable to use the toilets.

After we had eaten, we went to a pub, where there was an accessible toilet, and by then, it was welcome and necessary. The pub was quite busy; the accessible toilet was on the ground floor, but the other rest rooms were on the first floor. This meant most people needing the loo used the accessible toilet on the ground floor.

I don't have a problem with this because my opinion is it is a toilet that has been modified to enable people in wheelchairs to use it, but it is not necessarily for the exclusive use of wheelchair users. Despite this, each time I went to the toilet, everyone who came out of the toilet and passed me waiting in the queue to go in apologised. Even the very loved-up couple that came out of the loo together apologised.

Where an accessible toilet is available in a restaurant, bar, or café, it is quite often used as secondary storage. This means you can get in the door but can't get around the high chairs, mops and buckets, crates of soft drink, and similar that are also in there. At a place where we go quite often, there is a very good accessible toilet but difficult to get to because the corridor leading to it is where the high chairs and spare stools are stored.

I would point out this is not a malicious act against people in wheelchairs but more of a lack of understanding about what being unable to walk or stand means and what the limitations actually are.

The only thing I can do to avoid the problem is to research the venue before going and seeing if there are appropriate facilities there. This includes access to the front door, height of the tables, accessible toilets, if the bar service or wait staff are behind a tall counter I am not easily seen.

When visiting friends and relatives, I have been pleasantly surprised when they let me know they have looked at their bathroom or en suite and think it will work for me. Often we have been sent photos of the bathroom to check that it will work. This has happened a number of times now, and I am touched that consideration for my needs is important to others.

Another friend of mine had seen a ramp I had bought and decided the same thing would work at his house to get me up onto the verandah and into his house. He asked me to buy the ramp for him and gave me the money. I now get into his house easily using that ramp.

I was invited to a friend's 60th birthday celebration, which was held at his daughter's house. He contacted me before the party to let me know he had reserved a spot on the driveway for me to park so I had ease of access into the house.

My main take from this is my friends do not see me as disabled, although they are aware of my limitations and will accommodate them as best they can. They will have fun at my expense, but it is not malicious but more of a way of showing they care for me and will not treat me differently than any other friends.

I see this as healthy and right, and I am fortunate enough to have many such friends.

Chapter 14

Fitness, exercise, and training

Maintaining fitness is an incredibly important part of managing my disability. To a large extent, staying reasonably fit can minimise the effects of HSP. I am not saying keeping fit will get me walking again, but I can say keeping active and maintaining a level of exercise helps with many other health concerns, which can arise if you are in a wheelchair for the majority of the time. This includes things such as cardiovascular wellness, which can be adversely affected when the breathing, and heart rates do not increase "normally" as you are unlikely to spend the amount of energy required. Also, the postural impacts of sitting constantly can result in chest infections becoming worse quickly because of the restricted chest movement.

Similarly, when the appetite remains but activity reduces, there is a tendency to gain weight, which also effects cardiovascular health and conditions, such as diabetes, and blood pressure and kidney function can be compromised. There are probably a whole lot of things that can get stuffed up when you don't exercise, drink enough water, eat the right food, etc, which is often the effect a disability can have on you.

Understanding this is important for your continued health and well-being. There are a number of stressors that developing a disability will have on you. Mental health can be impacted in the majority of us who have developed a disability, either over time as I have done or those where a sudden trauma results in the disability. It is not uncommon for the accumulation of difficulties to seem overwhelming and for self-esteem, self-worth, and self-confidence to be undermined. With the additional worries created by toilet needs, financial stress, and the many simple tasks that have become more difficult, these can lead to depression. This can become severely incapacitating.

I have mentioned several times I am within a warm and loving family, which has helped me avoid a number of these effects. I have still experienced concerns over my self-worth, which has shaken my self-esteem, and I have questioned my perceived value. I have resolved these for the most part, but there is still a foreboding about what will come next.

This will probably never completely go away, but by understanding what is happening and factoring in my age, I continue to exercise, drink water, and eat appropriately, which is helping me retain a good level of fitness and maintain my health, which, in turn, supports my mental health.

Before I started developing HSP, I was guilty of not paying a lot of attention to fitness over the years because I considered myself to be reasonably fit and fairly active. This was somewhat delusional on my part because I did carry a fair bit of extra weight, my ability to climb hills seemed to be less than it was, and I found my clothes seemed to be getting more close-fitting, and I could no longer blame the washing machine for shrinking them.

Several years before I knew about HSP, I started watching what I was eating, walking more, and did some bike-riding, which ended up with me losing about 25Kg, which was a good result. Since the HSP journey began, I have kept the weight off and have managed to remain reasonably fit, which I need to do for a number of reasons other than those already mentioned. Regardless of how effortless it looks, pushing yourself around in a wheelchair is fairly easy when the ground is flat and level. Where there is a downhill slope, it is great fun to let yourself go and feel the wind in your hair and the thrill of going fast in a mildly out-of-control chair.

The reverse is not so true. Pushing the wheelchair uphill is hard work and can be very tiring, depending on the incline and how long the hill goes for. Slight inclines are not a big problem unless they are particularly lengthy, but the steeper they are, the harder it is to push yourself up.

I have mentioned the FreeWheel, which I use a lot when appropriate, but there are also other devices that can assist with rougher ground, such as off road wheelchair wheels, which have wider tyres and knobbly bits that help grip on gravel, dirt, or rougher ground. There are also all-terrain wheelchairs, which are basically a four-wheel drive chair that can be used on really rough ground. These are mostly powered chairs, but they can go virtually anywhere.

There are more robust chairs that use a self-laying track in the same way a bulldozer or tank uses. These look like a lot of fun, but so far, I have not been in one.

Ultimately, for a lot of reasons, it pays to stay as fit as you can when using a wheelchair, which helps in keeping your independence and enabling you the freedom to go wherever you can. The consequences of not maintaining your fitness and strength will be a lessening of your independence and more reliance on other people, such as family or carers, to travel with you so they can push the wheelchair for you.

This is not what I want for me until it is absolutely necessary.

We are members of a local gym where we go on a Saturday morning to get fit and perform some exercise. Getting there and back is an interesting family outing.

The gym is just on 2.5 kilometres from home, and unless it is raining, we walk there, although I, of course, roll. I attach my FreeWheel when we go to the gym, and once there, I simply unscrew the FreeWheel attachment to allow me to use the gym equipment.

The trip to the gym is mainly downhill, which has the benefit of allowing gravity to power the chair and makes the trip fairly simple. I also meet many people on the footpath or in a park I go through, and there is always a quick hello, nice-day, and so on, which is good.

One of the interesting bits is when going downhill fairly quickly, it is necessary to slow down and let people know you are coming through. With the prolific use of mobile phones and ear buds, many of the people I come up behind have no idea I am there, and when I come alongside them and say "excuse me" while I go past, many of them get a fright and jump. Most see the funny side of it, and so far, I have not had to call for medical assistance for any of them.

The funniest part of this is people walking dogs. Dogs seem to have a 360-degree awareness, so when I come along behind a dog, they turn around and look backwards at me. They will often stop, which makes the person walking them realise I am there also. We sometimes end up having a bit of a chat as I go past them. So far, the dogs have only been curious, and there have been some very large dogs that have come up for a sniff and a pat.

Once we get to the gym, we exercise, and then it's time to go home. We get coffee and then walk home together, which is good because it is now a 2.5-kilometre uphill trip, so my wife and daughter take turns pushing me up the hill. I do assist by pushing the hand rims around, but I am not sure if that helps much because the other two are puffing and panting and leaking sweat all over the place by the time we get home.

While talking about animals and wheelchairs, I have had some interesting interactions with them since I started using the wheelchair. A few years ago, we did a fundraiser for the HSPersunite group to help fund research into HSP. We decided to do a marathon along a local rail trail, and to get ready for it, we spent a few weeks walking along the track to get an idea of the route to take.

A marathon is roughly 42.2 kilometres, so we needed to get some training in before we did the actual trip, and we also needed to get sponsors. We did all this, and from the several practice runs, we determined how to cover the distance without too many hills to climb.

When we were out walking the route, we met some lovely people also riding bikes, walking, running, and even some riding horses. Everyone is friendly and asks how we are going and what a lovely day it is. There are a couple of places to get a coffee and a very nice pub along the way, which we visited several times. While the weather was nice, our practice sessions were a thoroughly enjoyable outing. We were often accompanied by friends and family, so it was a lot of fun.

On one occasion, we were walking along the track, and a young lady riding a horse was approaching us. The horse saw the wheelchair and stopped. There was no way the horse was moving, except to turn around and get away from me as fast as possible. The poor girl riding the horse had to get off and calm the jittery thing down. She took the horse off the track and gave us a very wide berth, and as they went past us, the horse was very nervous and panicky. We, of course, did the right thing and stopped moving while they went past, and once OK, the young lady apologised that her horse was afraid of us and then rode away again.

On another occasion on the same track, a few cows came over to the fence to check out the weird guy on the chair. We have been stared at by alpacas, sheep, cows, kangaroos, emus, possums, horses, kookaburras, waratahs, eagles, hawks, crows, magpies, and many others.

It is wonderful to be out in the countryside and experiencing all these different animals along the way. We have even seen a snake or two, but we tend to let them move away so we can avoid them.

The day of the marathon came, and the 30-plus-degree weather we had been training in disappeared, and Melbourne had more rain in one day than it had had at any time over the past 18 months. It was cold and wet, but we still did the full distance and raised about $15,000 for the HSP Research Foundation. The only animal we encountered on the day was a cow, ruminating as we went past and, I am sure, thinking we were insane wandering about in the rain. It was a lot of fun preparing for the day, and we all got a great sense of achievement from doing it.

The wheelchair cushion, however, took about a week to dry out.

I have used a fitness tracker to measure my steps and exercise, but none of them have lasted for longer than a few years before starting to play up. The last one I had also measured heart rate, but that stopped after a couple of years.

I really like the fitness tracker app, which is very clear and has a history you can look back on.

I now use a smart watch, and this has lasted well, although the app is not as well developed as the fitness tracker app.

It is still good to measure the steps taken and sleep times, etc, but it really only provides a measure against a target you can set.

There are also the little things I find amusing, but that is just me. Every so often, there is a picture that appears of a person going for a walk with the caption "Time to get moving" or, my favourite, "Let's go for a walk." There is no response from the watch when I say "no."

The watch and the link to my mobile phone provide some good information about my activities and measuring them, but there are some facets of the systems I am unable to use effectively. There is a place where your weight can be recorded, but because I can't stand up and stay still for anything more than a couple of seconds, and even then it is a bit risky, I am not able to achieve a weight reading on the scales. I can use the weight I was when I last weighed myself, but that is about three years ago now, and I have been told I have lost weight since then.

The other thing my watch measures is my heart rate, which is fascinating. I am now taking medication to address my atrial fibrillation and discovered the watch can also perform an ECG. This is amazing, and so about ten times a day, I am performing an ECG because I can. I am starting to wind this back a bit now, but that is only because the ECG takes a chunk out of the battery life. Also, the results are not all that I expected. The goal is to have the ECG come back with "Sinus rhythm," but for a number of reasons, the most common result is "Poor reading" or "Inconclusive"; neither of which are particularly informative. I do get the occasional sinus rhythm result, which is good because that is what we are aiming for. The other results are designed to be a concern for my wife. I will discuss this with the cardiologist when next we meet, but in the meantime, I will not worry about it because when all is said and done, I am using a watch to get the result. Oh, and I can also tell the time by looking at the watch as well.

In keeping with staying fit, I have been availing myself of the services of a personal trainer, who is very passionate about her clients' fitness and its maintenance. She assesses your capability at each session and designs workouts and which machine to use that will give the most benefit. She works with you on what you hope to achieve and then designs a regimen to get you there.

On top of that, she will also decide what is good for you and will introduce other exercises to address these additional requirements. She may not tell you about them, however.

I refer to her as the "Princess of Pain" because she insists if you do not hurt the day after the exercise, she has not done a good-enough job. Her goal is to have warm ears the morning after the workout because the cursing she gets from her suffering clients will be reflected by her warm ears. You will be familiar with the expression "my ears are burning," meaning someone is talking about you. I am sure some mornings she will need to bathe her ears in cold water because I have cursed her long and loud.

I am impressed by her tenacity and her thoughts around what regime we should follow to achieve what I need to achieve. My wife and daughter also work with her, and their fitness is improving as well. It seems to be a thing with her that there is a need to exercise your bum, glutes. There seems to be an increasing focus on this, and although it is not a big thing for me to work on because I sit on mine, it is a big deal for the others who groan and complain about having a sore bum and blaming this on the trainer as well.

She also uses a range of the gym equipment as part of the training, and with me anyway, she uses various resistance bands I need to pull on as part of my exercise. She has at times brought them out with a grin and slapped them down onto the floor, so I have modified her name to "Madam Lash, Princess of Pain."

I must admit to having a lot of fun at her expense. For example, because I have limited movement in my legs, she will help me use the leg press by lifting my feet into position on the end board and then hold them in place by climbing onto the bottom of the leg press so she can hold my feet where they need to be with her thigh. She then puts her fist between my knees to keep my legs apart instead of closing against each other, which is what they will do if left to themselves. I have commented she and I have a strong physical relationship and that my wife and I do not get this close. Not strictly true but worth the fun of it.

Recently, I was on the leg press, and she had my feet held up by her thigh as usual and her fist between my knees when she looked up at someone, smiled at them, and winked. I said this was quite unacceptable and that she should not stand there winking at other people with her hand between my legs. She did say because she was already smiling, she had to say hello somehow, and waving was not an option, so she winked at them. This only goes to show that the most innocent action can be misconstrued if the description uses terms that carry innuendo. Basically, we have a slightly grubby sense of humour.

We tend to discuss the limitations my condition imposes on me, and she thinks it would be hysterical if one day she had me fall out of my wheelchair at the gym and have her stand over me yelling for me to get up and stop being a wimp. She wants to see the reaction this will cause in the other gym members.

Having previously fallen out of my chair, the panic generated by people witnessing me on the ground is nice in some respects but really funny in others. You get the "Oh my god, that disabled guy has come out of his wheelchair. Now what do we do—shall we help him up, or do we ignore it?" Most of the time people will come and assist. On occasion, someone will ask what they can do to assist, which is preferable.

Madam Lash, Princess of Pain is also a teacher at a local school and has used me as an example with her students. She has told them of the exercises I do and the threat of leaving me on the floor and shouting at me. There did not seem to be any reaction to this until she mentioned I was in a wheelchair, at which point there was shock, horror, and then amusement. So you can see she is a warped and twisted human being like the rest of us.

One of the things I use at the gym is an exercise bike, which is more of a recumbent device and not a bike per se. This is because the pedals are in front of you rather than under you. It can take a fair amount of time for me to get my feet into the pedals and tighten up the straps because if I don't, my feet fall out of the pedals, which defeats the purpose of using the bike. What is amusing, however, is the trainer will give me enough time to get myself sorted out, but she will come across and tighten everything up if I take too long or cannot do it.

Once tied into the pedals, I rotate them backwards, where there is little resistance, because the important thing is the movement that stretches my legs and hamstrings rather than resistance. Sitting in a wheelchair for most of my time means there is little stretching being done, and the bike helps stretch the bits that need it.

It is a source of amusement for her and me that when I move to a piece of equipment, I often need to adjust my shorts because getting off the wheelchair and onto another seat will often pull my shorts down a little, so to maintain my modesty, I need to hitch them up a bit. I do comment I need to maintain my modesty, which is considered funny by my trainer. After a few sessions, she commented to me I did not need to concern myself with modesty in the gym because looking around, there is no shortage of bum cracks and boob cracks being flashed around the place. While this is true, I did say I would much rather observe the lack of modesty where boobs are concerned and a lot less of the bum crack; too many plumbers at the gym I think.

Although, as an older male person, there is a small matter of what is acceptable and what is not at the gym, and while there are an awful lot of young people using the gym, many of the females in their 20s also seem to be making a fashion statement by wearing tight-fitting and revealing gym gear. A glance is acceptable, but anything longer than that is a bit creepy, so my trainer commenting on bum and boob cracks on display, while amusing and true, is not something that can be observed overtly.

The other thing about the gym is everyone is friendly, and people will often ask me if there is anything they can do to assist me or even just ask how I am, and some will stop for a chat. It is quite a social environment, and despite using a wheelchair, there are no issues similar to those experienced in other environments.

Another aspect of the gym is the music being played. I often find the music is very modern, quite loud, and seldom anything I would listen to by choice. The system does allow you to select songs you want to hear, but the control is too high for me to easily use. It is refreshing when an older someone puts in their selection of songs. Most of the time this is good and shows people still like the songs popular in the '60s, '70s, and '80s.

Chapter 15

Mental Health

In the past, mental health was not well recognised as a health issue, and expressions were used to explain away some of the peculiar behaviours we now know are caused by a range of mental-health conditions. Many of these can be treated and managed with the help of counsellors, psychologists, psychiatrists, and medications.

I had not considered my mental health when my journey with HSP began or for some time afterwards. Even now, I do not consider mental health as something for me to be concerned about, but for many reasons, I am more aware of it now than I used to be.

I first started to think about it when one of the people in the band asked me if I was OK. At the time, I responded I was OK, and he then talked to me about why he asked. This was before the RUOK campaigns started, but a friend of his, who had developed a serious health condition similar to mine, had difficulty coping with it, resulting in a tragic outcome.

We have experienced some mental-health issues within our family and are aware of how debilitating they can be. One of my children is training to be a clinical psychologist, so if we have any questions, we have someone to go to.

In my case, as I have mentioned, there have been times when I have questioned my self-worth and my worries and concerns over the impact

I have on my family. Putting this into a mental-health context, I have found, although I have concerns about the progression of HSP and how that effects my family, my concerns are normal for a person in my position. I do not consider them to be impacting my mental health, and I would be more worried if I did not have them.

I am a fairly typical male in his mid-60s, and like many others of similar age, I could not say I am in touch with my feelings. More recently, this has changed a little but not significantly.

There are days when I have had enough of getting in and out of the wheelchair, when I have trouble lifting something, or needing something from a cupboard that is out of reach; dealing with the frustrations of trying to get up a small step or having people step in front of you, coping with ramps for disabled people being used to leave bins, building materials, or as experienced several times, the ramp is closed because the windows above it are being cleaned.

Most people would not think about the effect this has on a wheelchair user because unless you use one, it would not be a consideration. For someone in a wheelchair, however, these things do matter, and while having any one of them occur is no big thing, having them all occur on the same day has a more significant impact.

There have been times where a few of these have occurred for me, and I have given up and gone home. I was frustrated and quite annoyed at the time, but I got over it. Other people in similar circumstances can be totally overwhelmed by it, which does have a detrimental impact on their mental health.

I have mentioned several times I am fortunate to be part of a loving and caring family and I have supportive friends. Having access to this support helps me when I am having a difficult day by providing encouragement and a perspective I may have missed.

Although I do not need the support very often, knowing it is available helps when things do build up and affect me.

I have been asked by several people about how having HSP and being in a wheelchair affects my mental health. I have frequently had people say to me, "It must be tough being in a wheelchair," or "I can't imagine how difficult things are for you." I understand why people think that, but I don't feel the same way at all.

I would have far more issues and life would be a lot more difficult if I needed but did not have a wheelchair. The real meaning behind these comments is using a wheelchair means life has changed, and you are no longer able to do things most people do. In their eyes, this is a terrible thing, so obviously, I must feel bad about it.

This can be true for a lot of people who experience HSP or other conditions that limit mobility, and this may be reflected in their mental health.

When I reflect on what I have done and enjoyed before HSP got me, there are many things I miss because they are beyond my capabilities now. Bush-walking and climbing hills, swimming at the beach, playing golf, going for a walk, and riding a bike are all things I can no longer do.

There are times when I would like to use a bush track, go to the beach for a swim, or go for a ride with the rest of the family and see a different landscape. There are occasions when the people I am with will go for a walk in the bush or climb a track to the top of the hill. I cannot go, but I encourage them to do these things while I stay behind or do something else until they return. I am the one who can't do it, but that shouldn't stop the rest of my family from experiencing it.

Although I cannot participate with them on these experiences, my mental health does not suffer. I can't change my capabilities, so I am unable to go with them, and while that can be disappointing and occasionally upsetting, these are normal emotions, and I do not dwell on them, nor do I give it prominence in my list of things I don't like about HSP.

I know there are others who find these limitations to be difficult to deal with and who do suffer anguish and distress because of them.

The thing that may impact my mental health is where I worry that my infirmities and inability to do certain things places a burden on my family. At the moment, this is not a big concern but is something that, when I think about it, does worry me.

I would say I do not have mental-health issues, although I do have the normal worries and concerns life brings. I do think a lot of this is because of my attitude regarding my HSP and my acceptance that I can do very little about it. I also think if certain events in my life had not occurred, my attitude may have been different.

Just before I started showing symptoms of HSP, Sonja and I had begun laying a floating floor in the house. This was well outside our expertise, but we started and were about 80% done, when Sonja's brother passed away unexpectedly. Not only was this a tragic event because he was very young, but it was also something none of us had thought about. Parents, we know, will pass away at some point, but we never consider a sibling passing away unless they are unwell. His passing caused all of us to reevaluate what was important in our lives.

Work and career had been important to me. Sonja was working and consolidating her role, the kids were at school, and suddenly, we were shown our world was fragile and could change in an instant.

We did finish the floor after a period of reflection and reviewing what was important to us. We did not do this formally by discussion, but we each came to our conclusions about what was important and what wasn't.

Career very much became unimportant for Sonja and I, but interestingly, we progressed at work. Our family and building experiences together became our priority.

It was shortly after this that my HSP symptoms started to show, and I have wondered if the effort involved in putting the floor down and the emotional impact of my brother-in-law passing away was what triggered the HSP.

I doubt this is the case, but I think I will always wonder if there was something that caused the HSP to manifest.

We are not over his passing, and he is still missed. As with everything else we have done with the other adversities we have faced, we keep going.

Chapter 16

Music and playing an instrument

I have played a musical instrument since I was about 12 years old. I started learning the violin, and then when I went to high school, I picked up playing the trombone.

I did get fairly proficient on both instruments and also taught myself the rudiments of guitar and piano, and I could sing reasonably well.

Over the years, I have played in several orchestras on violin and, in some instances, trombone. I have also played trombone in brass bands and big bands, and I have also sung and played guitar, poorly, in some dance/rock bands.

Basically, I like playing music, but when I moved from New Zealand to Australia, I did not join any groups immediately, and I didn't look around to see where I could play. This went on for a while, and I realised I had not played for 16 years. In 2003, a person I worked with, who played saxophone in a big band, invited me along for a play with his group, which I did and enjoyed it. I found, even though it had been 16 years, I did not embarrass myself playing, and the music was the sort I enjoyed.

While participating in this group, I realised I had missed playing in a group and decided I needed to take it up again. I went and bought a secondhand trombone and joined the big band.

I played in a brass band for about three years, but with the progress of HSP and my commitments with other big bands, I could not continue with the brass band. I now play in two big bands, which is a lot of fun, and both bands are quite good.

Playing the trombone was not adversely affected when I started using the walking stick because at that time, I was still relatively mobile and retained my core strength, so I could hold the instrument and play it whenever and wherever I was needed.

Whether the performance is in the open air or inside a venue, there is usually a stage of sorts set up to play from. These could be band rotundas, elevated stages at community festivals, and stages in theatres, dance halls, school halls, or similar, which required climbing on to or up steps to get onto the stage. None of this was a problem for me until I started to use the wheelchair, but even then, because I could still walk a bit, I could get myself onto a stage if it was only a couple of steps but would need someone else to carry the wheelchair up for me.

Now that I can no longer walk at all, getting onto a stage may be a problem, depending on how high it is. If it is a small raised dais I can bunny-hop the chair onto, then there is little problem, but if it is up a few steps, then some planning is required. Fortunately, where we play regularly, there is no raised stage, so there hasn't been a problem.

As I have already mentioned, people are great, and whenever I have needed assistance at a gig or rehearsal, it has always been offered. This is most often from the people who play in the band with me, but other times it is an audience member or someone from another band. Most of the time this means someone carries my trombone and mute case for me, but other times it may be setting up the music stands. One of the biggest helps is when the band layout is changed to accommodate my wheelchair. This can be as simple as changing the order of the trombones, but this will also impact the saxes. The layout of a big band is fairly traditional, depending on the number of instruments in each section. The usual format will have a rhythm section, trumpets, trombones, and saxes. When the band is set up, the instruments with similar pitches will be put close to one another. An example is the bass trombone and baritone sax tend to play in the same part of the band, so if we reverse the order of the trombones, we then need to restructure the saxes so the bass instruments remain close to one another.

The trumpets generally fit in wherever they are put, and we tend to keep the rhythm section together and either central to the band or off to one side.

The good thing is the bands I play in are used to me and the wheelchair, so we tend to work it out OK.

There have been a few minor dramas with my mobility problems getting in the way, but for the most part, these have worked themselves out. A couple that spring to mind where things didn't quite go as expected are worth a mention.

We used to play regularly at a venue in Chirnside Park, and I needed to get into the middle of the band for the part I played. This was not a problem initially, but when I started using the walking stick, it became something of a joke that I needed to get in first, which was fine. When we stopped between sets, I needed to get out again, which meant squeezing past the other instruments, chairs, music stands, past the drum kit, and then out to the bar. This worked mostly, and I never damaged anything, but once things started getting more risky with my walking and a fall could damage other people's instruments, I took a different route, which involved me getting out through the saxes, which would move out of the way to let me out.

At another gig, and before I was using the wheelchair full time, we provided the music in Yea for the reopening of the town hall. This gig required me to get up onto the stage where we played a couple of sets. When getting down off the stage, I waited for everyone else to move away before I got up and moved off the stage. I had already packed up my gear, but as I got up and moved towards the steps, my walking stick got tangled up in one of the curtains, and I fell onto the floor quite heavily. I had hurt my leg when I went down and was not able to get back up again. One of the organisers went outside, where an ambulance was parked, and the paramedics came in to see what I needed.

They decided I may have broken my leg, and there was no way for me to drive home, so they got a stretcher, loaded me onto it, took me out to the ambulance, and whipped me off to hospital for a checkup. I had organised for one of the other band members to drive my car back to their place, and I had a lovely ride in the back of the ambulance, chatting to the paramedics. I also had to ring my wife and let her know what had happened, so she met me at the hospital, where I was X-rayed, advised that there was nothing wrong and I had not broken my leg, and that I could go home.

This was a better outcome than I was expecting but not an experience I would like to repeat.

Nowadays, HSP impacts my ability to play, but I am working out ways around the issues. The main thing is my core strength has deteriorated, which means I can no longer hold the instrument up. I get around this by tucking my elbow into my hip to provide the playing stability necessary. The other impact is, because I sit all the time, I do not have the wind capacity to play loudly. Luckily, I can cover this by playing the dynamics which is fine for piano, or mezzo piano, mezzo forte, and forte, but getting up to fortissimo and louder maybe not so confident.

I am looking at ways of making this easier, and I am confident I will be OK with it.

I have played with the first big band for nearly 17 years, and about a year ago, I started playing in another big band. I had to wait until they changed venues before I could join because they rehearsed and performed on the first floor of a popular club, and there was no lift.

With great fanfare, I was told they had moved locations and that everything was now on one level, so I fronted up to rehearse with them. Once inside, everything was on the same level, getting inside was not quite so simple. There was a fairly large step outside on the path to get to the door going into the building and another fairly large step to get into the building. There was a group of willing helpers who assisted me getting down the first step and up the next step so I could join the rehearsal.

Fortunately, I found a better way out that does not have any steps so did not require an army of assistants for me to vacate the premises.

There has been a minor change to getting me into the rehearsal by having that door left open for me to use.

The groups I have been playing in also attend a number of jazz festivals around the place, and these are always interesting with many different music styles being played. There are many smaller groups, trios, quartets, etc, as well as larger groups. It is very normal for musicians to play in a band that is their main group but will also play or "fill in" with another band or smaller group. Often, at a jazz festival, a group may be short a bass player or drummer, so they will contact other groups to see if they can get someone to fill in for them.

I have played in a number of these smaller groups, which is always fun, but with my more limited mobility, the opportunity does not present itself as much as it did.

There are some absolutely first-rate bands playing in and around Melbourne, and I have been fortunate enough to listen to a few of them over time. There are a number of venues around that specialise in jazz, and I would very much like to go to their shows. Unfortunately, most of the venues do not have lift access to the different floors where the bands play, so I am not able to see them. Simply put, it is not commercially viable for them to install lifts and accessible toilets in their venues, not just because of the cost but often because the buildings are heritage listed, and some modifications are not approved.

I have been in touch with many of the venues, and although not catering for disabled people, just about all of them have said if I can get myself to the level where the band is playing, they will carry my wheelchair up. Nice offer but not really achievable at the moment.

Other venues are well set up to accommodate wheelchair users, but they don't have jazz playing there.

One of the good things about playing in a group is once on stage and set up, my wheelchair is not an issue. I am just another musician playing my part within the group, and what I am sitting on is immaterial.

This is one of the really good things about playing in a group. It does not matter what age you are, how competent you are, or even what instrument you are playing. Once you have your instrument out and the charts in front of you, you are part of the team and expected to play what is in front of you.

I recently played at a workshop made up of three different groups with very different music styles. Each group played their music genre individually, and then we all came together for a piece, which had been arranged for the combination of the three groups. The three groups were a small jazz group, an orchestra, and a choir. The orchestra had many players in their '60s and '70s, but one of the violin players was a boy of 10 or 12 years old. He was as integral to the orchestra as anyone else playing, and even though he was significantly younger than everyone else in the orchestra, he was an equal player to everyone else.

I enjoy playing in the various groups and with the different ages of musicians. There are a number of players in their '80s who play in the band with me and also some who are still in their teens, but we all play the same stuff, and as a group, we do pretty well. There was a sax player, who was about 97, who sat in with us many times, who although not loud, could certainly play well. He had many stories about his playing experiences and was fascinating to listen to.

There are many musicians around, and certainly, many would be considered disabled in one form or another. Although there are several with a physical disability, there are many more who have a mental-health condition. For most, the playing and mutual support available in a music group provides an outlet and a focus away from their health issues, which is therapeutic and valuable to their well-being.

Chapter 17

Drinking and the effects of Alcohol

It is true that I have enjoyed a wee tipple since I was about 15 years old. Initially, this was because it was forbidden; the drinking age in New Zealand at the time was 20, but my friend looked older, and we could get beer at one of the local pubs.

As a normal healthy Kiwi male, I had a desire to fulfil the expectations of my peer group and drink myself into a coma at every opportunity. I did have some success at this, which was a likely source of deep concern for my parents.

Without going into too much detail, I did have some less-than-wonderful experiences brought about by my somewhat excessive binging, mostly to do with regurgitation, but once necessitating my father to purchase another car.

Once I started experiencing the symptoms of HSP, however, alcohol had a greater effect on my ability to walk. As you would be aware, when you have imbibed a few drinks, it is not uncommon to stagger a little and to feel the effects on coordination.

When you have HSP, you already stagger, and your coordination is affected. Adding a few drinks does not improve this but does, in fact, enhance the effect. When I could still walk using the walking stick, there were no serious problems; however, once I was using the wheelchair, although I did not stagger, I did find the effects on coordination were increased. This was not a problem for the most part but did cause some concerns with using the toilet.

Over the years, my reaction to drinking has changed, and I now enjoy a drink as much as I ever did, but I now limit myself because I am no longer able to manage the effects.

I live with a family who like to have a drink, but we are all good at stopping when we should.

One of the aspects I have admired in my children is the concept of drinking and driving is not a problem for them or their friends. If they are going out somewhere and intend to drink, they will either travel with a designated driver or use Uber. If they take their car, they do not drink. The maturity shown by this attitude is admirable, and further to this, there is no pressure on the designated driver to have a drink.

There is a definite negative perspective when we talk about drinking and alcohol, but this is not the only viewpoint. There is also a positive perspective for drinking, and for me, the benefits are not so much the effects of alcohol on my system but are more to do with relaxing and the social aspects. We have identified the drinks we like and stick to them.

Near to where we lived in Mulgrave, there is a reserve, Mulgrave Reserve, which is within walking distance from home. There is a local football team that uses the playing field and also has their clubrooms on the grounds. One of their players was a musician and organised a couple of concerts there to raise money for the club. They did really well and had some quite big names play there. In 2014, we went with a couple of friends and had a great time listening to the bands playing with a few hundred other people. There were food and drinks available, and the weather was good.

The following year, it was a bit bigger and well organised, and there were plenty of food tents as well as wine and beer sales. The music was really good, and the friends we went with enjoyed themselves immensely. With me in the wheelchair, getting around the place was a bit difficult because of the grass and the number of people there, but my friend pushed me when necessary.

We also discovered there was no glass allowed on the oval, so any wine purchased needed to be put into a plastic carafe and was drunk using plastic wine glasses. We were unaware of how many carafes we drank, but it ended up being more than one each. A carafe held a bottle of wine.

As you would know, when quaffing quantities of liquid, the human body processes it fairly quickly, and the alcohol component gets transferred into the blood stream, which sometimes distorts your ability to process information and also allows random ideas to take on a greater veracity than they actually deserve. The other effect is the liquid component gets processed by the body and produces pressure in the bladder, which needs to be released regularly.

Being on a sports ground, these needs were addressed using a series of "portaloos," which were certainly getting a lot of attention from increasingly inebriated concert attendees. Unsurprisingly, I needed to avail myself of these facilities, and my friend and drinking companion offered to push me across the grounds to them.

I was in no condition to refuse the kind offer, and so we set off across the playing field and down a slight hill on our way to the portaloos. At the bottom of the hill, there is a dip where the runoff water accumulates. There was no water in it at the time, but travelling in a wheelchair at faster-than-walking pace, there can be consequences, which we became aware of quite unexpectedly. When you get to the dip, the front castor wheels dig in suddenly, and their forwards motion ceases. Unfortunately, the person in the wheelchair maintains their momentum, which culminates in them leaving the seat and ending up lying on the grass. This happened going to the portaloos and returning from them. Fortunately, I was able to get back into the wheelchair without a problem, and there were enough people having a laugh at my dilemma but who were offering to assist.

When the concert had finished, we headed home. This was a fairly reasonable walk of a little more than a kilometre, but the three of us were quite inebriated, while my friend's wife does not drink so was completely sober. Most of the walk home was on a track through the nature reserve, which follows the creek, but once out of the trees and under the road, you then start using the footpath.

We staggered along the footpath and then had to cross the road to get to the side upon which we lived. Remembering our somewhat alcohol-affected state, we crossed the road very safely and attempted to get onto the footpath on the other side. Of course, there is a cutaway on the corner so wheeled devices, such as prams, kids' bikes, shopping trollies, and wheelchairs, can get off the road with little inconvenience.

When the person pushing the wheelchair is pissed, however, they may not take the same precautions necessary when regaining the footpath. When moving from the road onto the footpath incautiously, the same effect occurs, where the front castors stop moving but the person in the seat continues on. This happened, and I ended up lying on the footpath with my wife and friend laughing so hard, they were crying, while our sober companion lost it and became angry at her husband for trying to assassinate me. The funniest thing was the people living in the houses nearby came out to see what the noise was about, cars were stopping to see if the disabled guy was OK, and we could not stop laughing.

We all got ourselves together and continued to our home. When we got there, I was pushed along the path between the house and the garage to the bottom of the steps that led up to the front door. I was unceremoniously pushed to one side, while everyone else went inside the house for a nice cup of tea.

I, on the other hand, wondered how I was going to get into the house now that I had been abandoned in the shadow of the garage. I was still able to walk a few steps, but in my mildly inebriated condition, it would have been unwise to attempt the steps.

My daughter came out to see what I was doing and asked me how I was going to get inside. It was an interesting question because it became obvious she had no intention of assisting me into the house but was more inclined to offer advice and commentary on my efforts.

In the end, I got out of my wheelchair, and my daughter carried it into the house, whereupon I climbed the steps on my bum until I got into the house. I then had to get up another two steps to get through to the kitchen, where everyone else had congregated.

Upon getting there, I was advised my tea was cold because it took me so long to get into the house.

We have laughed about this for several years now.

I particularly enjoy social gatherings at home, where our friends are with us and our children and their friends are also. There is beauty in the families and ages mixing together and sharing views, opinions, and experiences and also having fun at the kids' expense.

In reality, we are a normal family, just like most other families. We have a circle of friends, and we occasionally get together to celebrate something, such as birthdays, anniversaries, Oktoberfest, New Year, etc.

We all enjoy these gatherings, and we eat and drink and talk and listen to music and argue over the selection of tunes. One of the things I particularly like about these get-togethers is that me being in the wheelchair makes no difference to anyone apart from friendly joking at my expense; however, I can give as well as I get.

Ultimately, we all have experiences from our years, and it is good to share these with one another. Our children are building their experience bank, and they will remember the social gatherings we have had. In the years ahead, they may remember these fondly, or they may grimace at the memory of their parents' parties. Either way, the experiences are increasing, and the lessons are being learned.

It is our intention to continue building on these experiences for many years to come.

Chapter 18

Public awareness of Disability

There is an increased awareness of disability, especially over the last five or so years, and this awareness is now more widely understood since a wheelchair user has been named Australian of the year. It is great that much of the awareness has been through talking to people with disabilities rather than what has been the common practice of able-bodied professionals, such as OTs, physiotherapists, GPs, and researchers, who observe and then decide on what is needed for disabled people.

As a wheelchair user, I am often surprised at what has been provided to assist me. Quite often, the assistive features are not assistive at all, or they are fine if you can stand and walk a pace or two. One of the places I worked recently had quite a good accessible toilet, which I used a number of times. It did need me to leave the office where I worked, take the lift to the ground floor, navigate a door between the two banks of lifts, turn down a fairly narrow corridor, and open the sliding door to the toilet. I then needed to squeeze between the hand basin, the toilet, and shuffle about until I could get the sliding door closed. Locking the door required me to put the brakes on the chair, push the door with one hand, and locking the door with the other. It was not possible to lock the door any other way when in a wheelchair, and if you did not lock the door, it would slowly open. Although it worked, it could have been made much more simple to use.

Once I started using the walking stick, I also started to get people staring, avoiding me, but also people asking me why I used the stick. What I found most interesting about this was those who avoided me, looked away, or ignored the stick were generally from English-speaking backgrounds, whereas those who did ask were predominantly from non-English speaking regions. This was out of curiosity because I was a little different. They didn't want details, but they invariably offered to hold a door or assist, if I needed it. Those who avoided eye contact or stared would also offer to assist, if needed. All in all, people are helpful and pleasant.

I absolutely love the openness of children who are curious and ask questions. I have some wonderful Q&A sessions with four- and five-year-olds, who ask about why I am in a wheelchair. I answer truthfully, without the medical diagnosis, and once they know I can't walk, they will ask how fast I can go or if my mum has to push me like a pram.

I will often hear children ask their parents why I am in the wheelchair, and most of the time they will get a similar response. I was pleasantly surprised once when the mother of a small child responded to the question with "Why don't you ask him?"

Adults are a slightly different story. I have never encountered anyone who was openly hostile towards me, but many people's reactions are surprising and often incredibly funny, if you choose to look from the other side and not be offended.

I went with my wife to a clothes' shop to buy some jeans. I wheeled into the shop, and the young lady behind the counter asked me how I was and what she could help me with. I told her I was fine, thanks, and that I would like a pair of jeans. She then looked at my wife and asked her what size I took. My wife's response was "I don't know, ask him."

To be honest, I was a little disappointed about this, but having thought about it, I don't think there was anything to be upset about.

Putting myself in the sales assistant's position, she sees a guy enter the shop in a wheelchair, and she may have no experience with wheelchairs or disabled people. Her thoughts are something like, *OMG, the guy is in a wheelchair. Why? Can he talk? Is he deaf? What else is wrong with him? How do I find out? Does he wear nappies? Will he smell? What do*

I say to him? Oh thank god, there is someone with him who looks normal that I can talk to.

There is no lack of wanting to help and sell the clothing, but not knowing what the person in the wheelchair is capable of can be quite confronting. I have experienced similar in medical facilities and hospitals, where there is experience with wheelchair users.

In general, I have found the average person will notice someone in a wheelchair and will attempt to stay out of the way. Until you get to a pedestrian crossing controlled by lights, then it's all on. Everyone crossing needs to get to the front of the crowd so they get across the intersection as quickly as they can. To achieve this, it is necessary to step in front of anyone you can get past and definitely get in front of the guy in the wheelchair because they will only slow you down.

Then once the light changes and they can cross, they have to get moving and try to get in front of everyone else also crossing, at the same time talking or texting on the phone. Then once they get across the road, they need to stop and look around to see where else they should go while also stopping anyone else from getting off the road. Once I get across in the wheelchair, I am polite and will ask people to step aside, and when they don't, I will nudge them gently until they do.

I also find it interesting how disabled people deal with one another. Meeting other people using a wheelchair does not immediately provide an opportunity to meet and chat about wheelchairs in very much the same way two-able bodied persons will not stop and chat about shirts, cars, etc.

I use a wheelchair, but I am not blind, deaf, and cognitively impaired. I don't have Parkinson's disease or multiple sclerosis, cerebral palsy, or other conditions. I, therefore, do not have an understanding of these other conditions and the limitations these may bring. I do know people with these conditions, but I cannot know what they are going through.

I was fortunate enough to work with a company that did some research into the needs of people with disabilities, and one of the people who worked on the project was blind and used a service dog. She posed a very interesting question to the group, which was "How many of the group used assistive technology?"

It was a very interesting question. I did because I have a wheelchair. She did because she had a guide dog. But we were the only two in the group who put our hands up. She than asked how many wore glasses for reading or distance, and most of the group did. She then pointed out glasses are assistive technology. Hearing aids are assistive technology. Without this technology, it would be difficult to function and continue working effectively. It was a definite light-bulb moment because there are many people who use a hearing aid, and we all know someone who needs or uses glasses.

Suddenly, assistive technology had a whole new dimension. Glasses enable you to see properly when your eyes no longer perform effectively, which is exactly the same as a wheelchair enables you to be mobile when your legs no longer work effectively.

Interestingly, at the end of the research, we gave a presentation to the group, and one of the guys I had been working with did the presentation. He started off talking about what we found out about the issues facing disabled people. He was immediately stopped by the senior manager who told him we cannot refer to the subjects as disabled people because they are "people with disabilities." I later told him it was good he had given the presentation because I would have referred to nuffies, which would probably have got me fired.

I have offended a number of people with my reference to nuffies, but they have mainly been people who work as nurses or carers and who are very conscious of the correct terminology. It is a term I no longer use. Although the term is not meant to be, it is often taken as disparaging or insulting and can certainly be a trigger for someone with a disability who was teased or bullied because of it.

In a lot of respects, it is good we are becoming more aware of how we discuss disabilities and how we refer to people with disabilities. The number of people who have a disability is surprising, and regardless of political correctness, a terminology not negative, discriminatory, or condescending needs to be found.

I was in Brisbane on a work trip and went for a wheel around the area. The weather was good, it was warm, and it was great to be out and about looking at different shops, cars, people, and things when between meetings. It was the middle of the day, and there were the usual lunch time crowds, so as I was rolling along the footpath, a young lady, probably late teens, came around the corner towards me. She had another person with her who was holding her arm because the young lady was vision-impaired and was using a white stick and being trained on how to use it.

As she came towards me, I moved over to the left side of the footpath, but as we went past each other, her stick got caught in my wheel, which startled her. The woman who was assisting her reassured her all was OK but that the stick had been caught in a wheelchair. I checked that all was OK, and the trainer said it was a good learning exercise because for a blind person, the stick is what gives perspective about where they are and that wheelchairs, prams, bikes, skateboards, and other people are normal things to encounter and that learning about them early on is good.

These are things I, as a wheelchair user, do not need to consider, and it absolutely brought home the fact that I may understand what it is like to not have working legs, but I can see and hear what is going on around me, whereas a person who is vision-impaired is navigating a very different environment from me.

There is also a perception in the general population that it must be dreadful to have a disability and that sympathy is necessary. This is so not the case for many with a disability. In my case, there are plenty of things I miss from when I could walk and some of the things I used to enjoy, such as bush-walking, exploring off the track, riding a bike with the family, and reaching the top cupboards in the kitchen. As I have mentioned in this book, the form of HSP I have is not too bad, and there are still many things I can do, so sympathy is wasted on me. Understanding what motivates people will also provide a perspective on why people say what they do when talking to people who are disabled.

I recently had a wheelchair loader, Abiloader, installed in my car. This is a device that takes the wheelchair from the rear of the vehicle and puts it down beside the driver's door. It also can pick up the wheelchair from the driver's door and put it away again in the back. It is a brilliant piece of engineering, and I have had many people comment on it and ask me about it. The reasons for people finding out about it or commenting are really quite interesting.

One couple saw me using it in the car park of the local shopping centre and stood and watched as I unloaded the wheelchair. Once I was in the chair, ready to wheel into the shops, they were asking me about the loader, where I got it from and more because they had a friend who needed something similar and wanted to know more about it. In the end, they filmed me getting back into the car and using the loader.

Another time, a family with young children stopped for a look and commented on the loader. They were mainly responding to questions from the child, who was also asking me questions. It was good, and we all went away happy.

Another occasion was outside the gym I attend, where an elderly couple came out of the coffee shop and told me what a wonderful technology this was and it must make my life so much easier and I can do things all by myself now. There was nothing wrong with this, but the way it came across was that I was a poor bugger who couldn't walk, but there was some technology that helps me a bit.

I would say my experience of people since I have been using the wheelchair is there are very few people who are unwilling to assist if they can, but many do not know how they can help. The main problem most people face is how to speak to someone in a wheelchair. I am often asked by people in the street if they can help push me across the road or up a hill or through a door. The beauty of this is people think about what may help me, and they ask. If I accept, then things happen, and I am grateful. If I don't need it, I thank them for the offer but decline.

The other side of this is, if I do need some help, I will ask someone if they can assist, and although I don't need this very often, when I have needed it, I have never been refused.

In general terms, people are great, and my experience has been very positive, until we talk of car parks, which I have discussed previously in this treatise.

We recently had family from overseas stay with us, and we took them around the area and did some touristy things with them. One of these was going to Phillip Island to see the Penguin Parade. On the way, we stopped at San Remo to see the pelican-feeding, which occurs at noon each day. I am unable to get onto the beach for this, but there is a place where you can see the show from a grassed area overlooking the beach. I found a spot where I could see from my wheelchair, but because the fence is on a concrete base, I was not able to get right up to the fence, so I got as close as I could and looked from there. This was working well initially, but once the feeding started, people began arriving and lining the fence to see. My view, as a result, got narrower but was still OK. An older lady using a walking frame sat nearby and then stood up and took her place at the fence. From that point on, I had no view of the pelicans at all.

I do understand people will get as close as possible to the action, but what I was quite disappointed about was at no stage did anyone consider if the guy in the wheelchair was able to see what was going on. Worse was nobody asked or even considered asking. I was completely ignored, and even when I attempted to move closer, I was actively blocked by people moving in front of me.

We travelled to several destinations around the state and had a great time and saw some amazing sights, including bushland, coastline, hills, and desert. At one point, we did some wine-tasting and ordered some tasting platters. This was very good and enjoyable. There was a birthday party on at the same time, so there was quite a crowd. A man in a motorised wheelchair went past us and a bit later stopped and asked why I was in a wheelchair. We had a discussion about our conditions that required the wheelchair. My condition of HSP was related to the condition he had, but the outcomes for each are very different. He had motor neurone disease, which is a terminal condition, but he had already outlived the expected time frame and was still talking and had an appetite for food; he had just finished a steak.

He was looking for the accessible toilet but had not found it. When he came back, I asked if he had found it OK, and he said yes, but his chair was too big to get through the door. Unperturbed, he said he would just have to wait until he got home.

Perspective is an interesting part of having a health condition, and while my HSP has certainly impacted me and my family, his condition has a far worse outcome, and the degeneration is more profound than what I will experience. Despite the inevitable outcome of his MND, he was a happy and agreeable person and had a positive outlook on things. Above all, he was enjoying himself and showed no resentment or anger at his condition.

It is an old joke, but it is quite accurate. I have been asked by different people about if I should be referred to as handicapped, disabled, crippled, and which I would prefer. My answer has always been that my name is Ted, and my preference is to be called Ted. The sad part of this is the person asking the question is often surprised by the answer.

I have seen a number of Facebook posts from other wheelchair users who are offended by the question. While I understand why offense is taken, I am not offended because in these days of understanding correct and non-pejorative ways of referring to individuals, groups, minorities, genders, ethnic groups, etc, people are genuinely concerned about using a term deemed offensive. People who know me have called me all sorts of things in reference to my use of a wheelchair. I now refer to myself as a wheelchair user who drives an accessible car and uses an accessible or disabled car park. I have modified how I refer to myself because a number of people have commented to me that the term I previously used was offensive. I still choose where I use the expression and have chosen not to use it here.

Chapter 19

NDIS

The introduction of the National Disability Insurance Scheme (NDIS) into Australia has been the most beneficial initiative for people with disabilities. It was recognised that having a disability and living with it had an impact on not only the individual with the disability but also on their family. Funding was introduced with a view to reduce the burden on family that a person with a disability may impose.

The costs my family have incurred since I started displaying symptoms of HSP have been significant, but since the NDIS took me on, a lot of the funding has become available to me. Some examples of the work needed that we have paid ourselves to accommodate my limitations are

- Modifications to the bathroom to enable a wheel-in shower, tiling and handrails for the shower and toilet
- Manual controls for the car
- Adding an opener to the rear door of the van
- Ramps needed around the house
- My first wheelchair

My second wheelchair, which I needed, was partially assisted by a Victorian initiative for people needing equipment called Statewide Equipment Program (SWEP).

As you can appreciate, these costs are only part of what a person with a more severe disability will require, particularly equipment, such as hoists, specialised vehicles, motorised wheelchairs, specialised chairs for those needing restraints, head braces, etc.

I have spoken to some people who have had very good experiences with the NDIS. One of these people had a son who was in a wheelchair but had an obsession with playing wheelchair rugby. This was unattainable until the NDIS came along, assessed the need, and funded the purchase of a chair for him.

In my case, I needed to get a wheelchair that suited my height and long legs, and so I was measured up, and a chair designed for me which was funded by NDIS.

I also have had difficulty getting my wheelchair in and out of the car, so with the assistance of an occupational therapist, we looked for solutions to the problem. In the end, the only product that would enable the chair to be accommodated in the back part of the van but able to be delivered to the driver's door was an Abiloader. The request was provided to NDIS, and after six months, the purchase was approved. This has been a wonderful assistance to me and has given me back a lot of independence and has enabled me to be mobile without needing anyone to accompany me.

Being in a wheelchair means there are a number of things I am unable to do around the house, such as lawn-mowing or house-cleaning, which the NDIS now funds for me. The funding is designed to make things easier for people with disabilities and to help make them less dependent on family members.

For those families where a person is living with a disability, whether physical, cognitive, or both, the NDIS has opened up the opportunities for their lives to be made a little easier without having a significant impact on the household budget.

I have a friend whose daughter was recently diagnosed with MS, and the NDIS has helped greatly with access to support funding, home assistance, vehicle modifications, etc. The beauty of it is that the quality of life for not only the person with the disability but also their family is preserved without the huge impact that purchasing the necessary services and equipment involves.

Although providing a huge benefit to people with disabilities and their families, it is not a perfect system and has been abused by many, which has had the unfortunate consequence of making things a little more difficult for participants and those trying to get onto the system.

There are a number of hoops to go through to apply for access to the NDIS, which includes obtaining letters from GPs, specialists, identifying and documenting the support needs, as well as other forms of supporting documentation. Once these are provided and accepted, there is an interview process where your needs are gone through and a plan created with funding for each area that is needed. This can take some time to arrange and schedule, and it is important for the participant to know what they wish to achieve.

The other consideration is time because it can take a relatively long time for the plan to be accepted and budgets established. In my case, it was several months from applying to getting interviewed and approved. Additionally, when looking to purchase capital items, such as wheelchairs, vehicle modifications, etc, the approval process can start with provisional approval being provided, but to finalise the acquisition requires obtaining and providing quotes to NDIS, which must be approved before a purchase can be made. This process can take many months or longer.

A purely personal observation is that many allied health services have become more expensive since NDIS was introduced. An example is the cost of an occupational therapist, speech therapist, physiotherapist, and similar, where the hourly rate has increased significantly even though the price has been set by NDIS. Although the prices were established as the maximum chargeable for the service, it has very quickly become the rate charged.

This has put the services necessary for those who do not have an NDIS plan out of reach.

Another effect is that accessing some services has become difficult because of the increased demand for service providers, such as occupational therapists, etc. Some professionals who are able to provide services have discovered that the process of gaining certification, which will allow them to work and be paid by NDIS, is complex and expensive. Many of these practitioners have not gone through the certification process, which means they cannot provide services to individuals who have their plans managed by the NDIA, a division within the NDIS. Those practitioners who are not certified by NDIS or NDIA can provide their services to participants but only if the plan is managed by a third-party plan manager or is self-managed by the participant.

I know of some participants seeking an OT to assess their accommodation, motor vehicle, and powered wheelchair needs facing difficulty in finding an OT who can do the work and will work on an NDIS-funded job in a reasonable timeframe. I had an example of this when looking for an OT to assess my vehicle. One of the people I contacted said they were qualified to do the work, were happy with NDIS funding, but could not schedule me in for at least 12 months. This is becoming a fairly common story and much more difficult in regional areas and extremely difficult for those in remote areas of Australia. Many assessments are now done via telephone or other technologies, which work quite well. Provision of services, however, are not always possible via video calls, although many are. Where this is the case, alternative ways of providing the services need to be found, which may involve travelling to access them.

The NDIS is a wonderful resource for people living with disabilities and provides the means for those needing services to be able to access them and to improve their quality of life. It is not perfect, and there have been some issues needing to be resolved. Ultimately, these are being worked through, and the system is improving, but it will take time.

Chapter 20

Experience with toilets

You will have noticed I have mentioned toilets and their use several times in this book. I have brought a number of my experiences together here. A toilet is something we all need to use, but for me, in a wheelchair, there are some requirements not available to me unless the toilet has been built with access in the design.

At home, the bathroom has been modified to meet my needs. When I was working, the toilets in the office also accommodated my needs, and as mentioned, if we stay in a hotel, motel, cabin, we ensure they too can meet my needs.

Public toilets, which we need when travelling, frequently have a toilet for disabled people.

I am of the opinion that accessible toilets are ones that have been designed and built so those who need them can use them. I do not think, however, they are there for the exclusive use of disabled people. If a person who is not disabled comes out of the accessible toilet, that is fine.

My only complaint about access to public toilets is they tend to be messy and often not very clean. More often than not, the floor is wet, the seat needs cleaning, and there is often nothing to dry your hands with after washing.

Some public toilets do not have a seat on them at all, and instead, there is only the metal rim, which is just dreadful, not to mention, yuk!

Most of the accessible toilets seem to have loose, broken, or unattached seats. Not normally a problem, but when you need to transfer from your wheelchair onto the toilet with a seat that moves too, it can be an interesting and sometimes quite a painful experience.

The facilities in smaller towns seem to be better maintained than those in the larger cities. Shopping centres, service centres selling fuel and food, McDonald's, and other fast-food outlets generally have accessible bathrooms usually reasonably OK to use.

Accessible toilets are generally unisex so are used by male and females and often are also the baby change room. This means there are receptacles for sanitary products, soiled nappies, and the usual rubbish bin in there also. For some reason, all these receptacles are placed near to the toilet, so when using the wheelchair and transferring, it is often necessary to move these bins out of the way. This is not a problem but can be frustrating if there are several that need to be moved.

Frequently, the accessible toilets are locked. This is the case for accessible toilets in many of the parks and gardens but also can be true for those located near public areas, such as beaches and picnic spots. As we have experienced in a number of places, the key to open the toilet is available from a kiosk or shop nearby. This is fine when the shop/kiosk is open, but if it is closed, access to the toilet is not available. Where there is no business nearby, the toilet is locked but can be opened with an MLAK key. This is a key that opens all public accessible toilets and is provided by the Master Locksmith of Australia. Anyone with a disability or their carer can apply for an MLAK so these toilets become available.

The need for the key means only people with disabilities can use these toilets. It is important and a matter of common courtesy that the person using the toilet leaves it in a condition that the next person can also use it. This will mean it is necessary to clean up after yourself. Unfortunately, this is not always the case, so on occasion, you may need to clean it before you use it.

In most cases, the accessible toilets are fine and in places such as shopping centres, malls, and high-traffic areas, the toilets are often maintained with attendants on hand. For the most part, accessing toilets suitable for people with disabilities is manageable and available in most places.

Chapter 21

Swearing and the use of profanity

When I was still at school, there was an incident I thought was minor but necessitated my parents meeting with the school principal (headmaster on those days) and my form master to discuss my continued attendance at the seat of learning.

Upon their return home, my father informed me I will continue to attend the school. He also added that the form master had advised my parents of an activity at which I excelled. Upon asking what that was, my father was informed, "I have never met a 15-year-old boy able to swear as eloquently as your son."

I did discover, although disapproving, my father was surprised and a little bit proud of this. It was not the use of swear words alone, but also the phrasing and supporting dialogue that made it outstanding.

Since those halcyon days, language has become important to me, and the art of swearing has been refined and become quite common. In fact, the use of the word "fuck" as a noun, verb, adjective, and pronoun has become normal in our family communications.

The word is referred to in many different ways, e.g., f***; F bomb, fark, feckn, or my favourite, the "dirty in-and-out word."

One of the positives of swearing is the therapeutic impact it has on your well-being. It has been identified that swearing can help reduce pain (Keele University research published in *The Journal of Pain*, 2011) and manage difficult emotions and frustration (Dr Raffaello Antonino, Therapy Central).

Since my HSP has progressed, there are many aspects of the condition that cause some anxiety and frustration. I find swearing provides me with some stress relief, manages my frustrations, and provides an outlet to express myself, normally said when on my own and when something annoys, frustrates, or otherwise engenders a negative feeling in me. My go-to phrase is "for fuck's sake," which has very little literary meaning and isn't even grammatically correct, but it does provide an immediate release, and I feel better.

Many other people derive the same benefits out of the use of profanity as I do. One of the people I worked with is a highly qualified IT person, whose phrase when frustrated or thwarted was "Fuck, fuck, fuckety, fuck, fuck, fuck." This was a phrase that allowed her to vent and get over the immediate issue while also being a source of amusement for the rest of us in the office.

I do think that in today's world the use of swearing is no longer a "shocking" thing and that most of us understand and accept its use.

When expressing yourself by swearing, it is sensible and polite to be aware of and accommodating of where you are and with whom. It may not be correct to swear in certain places or where certain people are present. For example, I seldom, if ever, swore when my parents were with me. If I did occasionally swear, it would be a word such as "bloody" or "bugger" but would not be the "dirty in-and-out word." Even so, it would still be met with a "tsk," a frown, or a more verbal chastisement, particularly from my mother.

As I have mentioned, times have changed, and the use of profanity is now more widely accepted.

On a side note, it is absolutely weird that news sites, web sites, and others will edit out or modify a swear word so you can tell what the word is but it is not actually printed, e.g., f**K or sh*t. Turn on the TV, however, and on many programs, these words are not edited, depending on the time of day they are broadcast.

Chapter 22

What the future may bring

Interesting concept really, what does the future hold for any of us? Clairvoyance is definitely not my forte, and very little is certain or definite in this life.

Many people, when discussing the future, will use the expression "you could get hit by a bus," which really means you cannot plan for everything and that unexpected things can happen.

This expression was used where I worked and particularly when discussing contingencies, reliance on specific personnel, documentation, and sharing the knowledge. What is the impact if you are suddenly not here?

The sales manager at the time did not like the expression because it was very negative, so she used the expression "when you win the lottery," meaning you are now rich and don't need to work anymore. A much more positive perspective but the result is the same: You will no longer be available at work.

The one thing that scares me the most about having this condition is the word "hereditary" in the name. I remember the anguish on my mother's face when I let her know I was showing signs of HSP, the same as my father had. I remember feeling guilty that I had caused Mum to be upset, and this continued on other occasions when I saw her. Progressing through the walking stick and into the wheelchair caused Mum more grief as I deteriorated, but she had also supported Dad through his journey through HSP and dementia, which ended in his death. I am sure she was seeing the same thing happening to me, but so far, this does not appear to be the case. I am also certain I have better medical expertise around me than my father had available to him.

I am dreading the day but hopeful it doesn't happen, that one of my children or grandchildren start showing HSP symptoms. That is why gene-testing is so important to me; it will identify if there is a possibility of HSP occurring in one of my direct descendants or if the gene is not evident, then HSP will not appear for that person or their children.

For me, there are some clues about what may occur over the next few years. Improvement is unlikely but could happen if the research identifies a way to relieve the symptoms.

It is possible that my condition will not progress any further, although unlikely.

It is also necessary to remind myself that HSP has certain symptoms, but I am also past 65, and there are some consequences of living a longish life.

I used to smoke cigarettes quite heavily and at one stage, was smoking about 40 per day. I have been a non-smoker now for over 30 years, so I am fairly sure the effects will have all gone by now. I do drink, although this has moderated substantially, but again, the effects may also contribute to my continued demise.

Mostly, though, I think age and physical decline will curtail some activities; however, I would like to think I can continue my music-playing for a good many years yet.

The recent fall in the shower, which hurt my shoulder, has taken several months to heal so far and is still painful, so I expect it will take a few more months before it becomes pain free. It is definitely improving but will take time, and I have been advised, even if I did not have HSP, at my age, the healing process for this type of injury would still be several months.

There is a list of things that may happen in the future, but without knowing what they are, there is no point in worrying about it, and as usual, we will cope or adapt as and when they do appear.

The progression of this condition in me is unknown, but there are some things that are highly likely and others that are possible but less likely and still others that are possible but unlikely.

The things that are highly likely are

- Further deterioration of mobility
    o   increased weakness in legs
    o   effect also occurring in arms
    o   continence issues, particularly bladder

Possible but less likely are

- Other symptoms beyond mobility:
    o   Major continence issues requiring catheterisation and/ or stoma
    o   Further deterioration of core strength affecting back and ability to sit upright
    o   Loss of sensation from waist down, requiring daily check for wounds, bruising, etc

Possible but unlikely:

- Cognitive degeneration:
    o   Dementia
- Sensory deterioration:
    o   Hearing loss
    o   Sight loss
    o   Loss of feeling in legs, hands
- Other possible issues
    o   Heart problems
    o   Spinal curving caused by sitting
    o   Pain and increased spasticity

Some of these possible further issues may be alleviated by increasing medication, particularly baclofen, and other aspects of the condition may be attributable to age rather than HSP; however, the differing forms of HSP can include a number of these symptoms.

As I have mentioned previously, my symptoms seem to be similar to others with HSP, but I do not experience debilitating pain. I hope this continues to be the case and that my symptoms remain as they are. I do have concerns that as my mobility deteriorates, I will need more assistance with personal care.

Because of the Covid pandemic, a number of things I used to go out to have done, I now do at home with assistance from my family. I bought a grooming kit so I can cut my hair. I did it myself a couple of times, but now my wife does it for me because she could not take the mess I made of it. As a consequence, I now have much shorter and neater hair than I used to have.

I use a manual wheelchair mostly, but I have a motorised wheel, which I use a bit when going long distances or where there are hills to climb. I can see me using this more as things progress and I become less able to push myself in the manual chair, but I hope to delay this as long as possible.

I have noted elsewhere in this book that HSP is one of the more obvious ailments that affect me. The impact is, of course, the inability to walk and my use of the wheelchair. I am also of an age where time is showing its impact on me also. There are lines on my face, thinning hair, a tendency to tell "dad" jokes, and a preference for '70s music.

I have referred to the lines on my face as laughter lines and are an indication of my amused attitude towards life and its effects on me. I was, of course, informed these can't be laughter lines because nothing is that funny!

Age is definitely something that will have its impact on my health and abilities, but despite knowing I am in late middle age, I still feel younger than my years. Age often comes with the deterioration of parts of the body, and this will occur but will not be caused by HSP. In some respects, having HSP can minimise some of the age-related conditions. This is because the management of HSP and the treatment of it can also slow the aging process for some areas. For example, pushing the wheelchair and transferring from it to other places has strengthened my arms. The gym and the trombone-playing help with my breathing, cardiovascular system, and overall fitness, all of which contribute to my continuing health and wellness.

As mentioned, knowing what the future may bring is not something that can be identified with any certainty. Some aspects of this condition are fairly likely to happen, but most are less certain and may not occur at all.

What I do know is whatever HSP brings my way, it will be managed and accommodated by Sonja and me. At this stage, there are plenty I am unable to do but still a great many things that I can do and am doing.

I fervently hope this is the case for many years to come.

Index